1 Corinthians

Books in the Bible Study Commentary Series

Genesis—Leon J. Wood
Exodus—F. B. Huey, Jr.
Leviticus—Louis Goldberg
Numbers—F. B. Huey, Jr.
Deuteronomy—Louis Goldberg
Joshua—Paul P. Enns
Judges—Paul P. Enns
Ruth—Paul P. Enns
1,2 Samuel—Howard F. Vos
*1,2 Kings—Howard F. Vos
*1,2 Chronicles—Eugene H. Merrill
Ezra, Nehemiah, Esther—Howard F. Vos
Job—D. David Garland
*Psalms—Ronald B. Allen
*Proverbs—Eldon Woodcock
Ecclesiastes—Louis Goldberg
*Song of Songs—Edward M. Curtis
Isaiah—D. David Garland
Jeremiah—F. B. Huey, Jr.
Lamentations—Dan G. Kent
Ezekiel—Paul P. Enns
Daniel—Leon J. Wood
Hosea—D. David Garland
*Joel—Ronald B. Allen
Amos—D. David Garland
*Obadiah, Jonah—John H. Walton and Bryan E. Beyer
Micah—Jack R. Riggs
Nahum, Habakkuk, Zephaniah, Haggai—J. N. Boo Heflin
*Zechariah—Homer Heater, Jr.
Malachi—Charles D. Isbell
Matthew—Howard F. Vos
Mark—Howard F. Vos
Luke—Virtus E. Gideon
John—Herschel H. Hobbs
Acts—Curtis Vaughan
Romans—Curtis Vaughan and Bruce Corley
1 Corinthians—Curtis Vaughan and Thomas D. Lea
*2 Corinthians—Bruce Corley
Galatians—Curtis Vaughan
Ephesians—Curtis Vaughan
Philippians—Howard F. Vos
Colossians and Philemon—Curtis Vaughan
The Thessalonian Epistles—John F. Walvoord
The Pastoral Epistles—E. M. Blaiklock
Hebrews—Leon Morris
James—Curtis Vaughan
*1,2 Peter, Jude—Curtis Vaughan and Thomas D. Lea
1,2,3 John—Curtis Vaughan
Revelation—Alan F. Johnson

*Not yet published as of this printing.

BIBLE STUDY COMMENTARY

1 Corinthians

CURTIS VAUGHAN
AND THOMAS D. LEA

**Lamplighter
Books** Grand Rapids,
Michigan
Zondervan Publishing House

Lamplighter Books is an imprint of Zondervan Publishing House,
1415 Lake Drive, S.E., Grand Rapids, Michigan 49506

1 CORINTHIANS: BIBLE STUDY COMMENTARY
Copyright © 1983 by The Zondervan Corporation
Grand Rapids, Michigan

Library of Congress Cataloging in Publication Data

Vaughan, Curtis.
    I Corinthians: Bible study commentary.

    Bibliography: p.
    1. Bible. N.T. Corinthians, 1st—Commentaries.
I. Lea, Thomas D. II. Title. III. Title: 1st
Corinthians, Bible study commentary.
BS2675.3.V38   1983   227'.207   83-21653
ISBN 0-310-44021-1

Edited by Edward Viening

Printed in the United States of America

87 88 89 90 91 92 / EP / 10 9 8 7 6 5 4 3 2

To Frances and Beverly

CONTENTS

Preface

This book has been designed to provide guidance for pastors and church members who want to understand better the meaning and message of 1 Corinthians. The content is a brief exposition that follows a simple outline of the writing. An effort has been made to follow the drift of the author's thought, pinpoint the chief themes of the book, and explain the meanings of important words and phrases.

We are indebted to several persons and institutions for their encouragement and assistance: Zondervan Publishing House for requesting the manuscript; the president and trustees of Southwestern Baptist Theological Seminary for providing encouragement and assistance in undertaking this task; and the following secretaries who assisted us at various stages of preparation: Mrs. Toni Hickman, Miss Pam McMurray, and Mrs. Sherrie Rapaglia.

Introduction

The Epistle called 1 Corinthians is the most practical lengthy epistle Paul penned. In its pages the apostle confronts and provides solutions for church divisions, discusses litigation between Christians, crumbling family life, disorders in public worship, and stinginess among Christians. He treats such moral failures as incest, homosexuality, and fornication. He defines the content of the gospel and underlines the centrality of the Resurrection. For good measure he also touches on the position of women in the church, the practice of glossolalia, and the nature of the resurrection body. Few modern churches confront the entire spectrum of problems that Paul met in Corinth, but there is enough identity between the failures of the Corinthian church and our own to provide help for many of the problems vexing congregations today.

The City of Corinth

The commercial importance of Corinth was due to its geographical location. It was situated on an isthmus linking northern Greece with the Peloponnesian Peninsula and could boast of two harbors, Lechaeum on the Ionian Sea to the west and Cenchrea on the Aegean Sea to the east (Acts 18:18).

Sailors could cross the narrow isthmus at Corinth and avoid the stormy Peloponnesus. Larger vessels unloaded passengers and cargo at one port and assured the passengers that another ship in which they could continue their voyage would be available at the next port. Some smaller ships were hauled overland by human hands utilizing a form of railroad composed of wooden rollers.[1]

The population of Corinth was transient and cosmopolitan. The city attracted many whose purpose for visiting was illicit pleasure. The name

---

[1]N. M. Verdelis, "How the Ancient Greeks Transported Ships Over the Isthmus of Corinth," *Illustrated London News* 231 (1957): 649–51.

of the city gave birth in the Greek language to many words that were used to express a life of luxury and licentious living. To be a Corinthian was synonymous with living a debauched lifestyle.

The outstanding physical feature of Corinth was the massive plateau known as the Acrocorinth which rose nearly 2000 feet from the surrounding land. At its foot the city of Corinth grew and flourished. Atop its flat summit some 1000 sacred priestesses in the service of Aphrodite, goddess of love, had made their services available as cult prostitutes.

The Roman conqueror Lucius Mummius had virtually destroyed Corinth in a battle in 146 B.C. The city was rebuilt by Julius Caesar in 46 B.C., and its favorable location again contributed to its rapid growth. During Paul's visit the population of the city is estimated to have ranged somewhere between 100,000 and 500,000. The temple housing the sacred prostitutes had been destroyed in the razing of the city by Lucius Mummius. The new Corinth did contain a temple, but it is not certain that the notorious temple prostitutes were present during Paul's visits. However, the immorality that had always been a trademark of the city was still its heritage.

In addition to its commercial importance Corinth was also the home of the Isthmian Games, the best attended of national festivals in Greece apart from the Olympic contests. These were held every other year in a suburb of Corinth, and many participants and visitors came to Corinth for these events. Paul's athletic descriptions in 9:24–27 may reflect the influence of these games.

Authorship

References to 1 Corinthians in early Christian writings are both early and frequent. In A.D. 95 Clement of Rome wrote to the Corinthians in the name of the Roman church and mentioned that the factious spirit evident in 1 Corinthians was still evident in the church to which he wrote (1 Clement 47:1–3). Ignatius and Polycarp freely quote from the book. Many early Christian leaders specifically attributed the book to Paul the apostle.

The claim for Pauline authorship in 1:1 is reinforced by a style and language that fit with the other accepted Pauline writings. The contents of the letter correspond with what we know of the situation that Paul would find in Corinth. The letter contains strong condemnations of the Corinthian church, but there is evidence that the church so treasured the writing that it was preserved and not lost as were some other letters by Paul.

Paul's Relationship to Corinth

In Acts 18:1–18 Paul's initial contact with Corinth includes the following sequence of events:

1. In Corinth on his second missionary journey Paul met Aquila and Priscilla, lived with them, and worked at tentmaking with them (18:2–3).

2. He preached each Sabbath in the synagogue (18:4). Eventually he was driven from preaching in the synagogue and moved into the home of a proselyte named Justus, who lived near the synagogue (18:6–7).

3. Crispus, a leader of the synagogue, and many gentile Corinthians were converted (18:8).

4. Paul was encouraged in his ministry in Corinth and received a vision from the Lord. He remained in the city for eighteen months (18:9–11).

5. The Jews brought Paul before Gallio, Roman proconsul of Achaia, and demanded that he be punished for his contentious teaching. Gallio saw their requests as a Jewish dispute, refused to involve himself, and allowed the gentile crowd to rough up Sosthenes, the leader of the synagogue, who had replaced Crispus (18:12–17).

6. Paul left Corinth, taking Priscilla and Aquila with him (18:18).

After leaving Corinth, Paul eventually left his friends in Ephesus, sailed to Caesarea, and then to Jerusalem. He later returned to Ephesus and remained there for nearly three years (Acts 18:19–19:10). In his absence the spiritual conditions within the church deteriorated greatly, and he may have received reports about this from friends in the church. When he returned to Ephesus, he likely wrote to them a letter mentioned in 5:9 warning the Corinthians not to associate with the immoral and the wicked. This letter has not been preserved.

From members of Chloe's house (1:11) Paul later learned that the church in Corinth had split into factions. He also received a letter from the Corinthians asking his advice and guidance on certain issues relating to the church (7:1). It is possible that a delegation composed of Stephanas, Fortunatus, and Achaicus may have brought these questions to Paul (16:17). On the basis of the reports and the request, Paul wrote 1 Corinthians and perhaps sent it to the church by Titus (2 Cor. 12:18).

Twice in 1 Corinthians (4:17; 16:10) Paul mentions sending Timothy to Corinth on a special mission. Paul's introduction of Timothy's name does not suggest that Timothy carried the letter, but it suggests that he was sent to handle some congregational problems that had occurred. Apparently Timothy was unable to handle the difficulty. Paul's authority was disputed (2 Cor. 10:10; 12:6–13), and Timothy returned to report this to Paul.

Date

The first arrival of Paul at Corinth and his appearance before the proconsul Gallio are mentioned in Acts 18:1–18. Fragments of an inscribed
stone found in this century at Delphi in Greece permit us to date the
probable service of Gallio as spanning the period from the summer of A.D.
51 through the summer of A.D. 52. The stone dates an order of the
emperor Claudius and refers to Gallio as the proconsul of Achaia.[2] We do
not know with certainty the time of Paul's appearance before Gallio, but it
is possible that Paul resided in Corinth from the spring of A.D. 50 until the
fall of A.D. 51 (Acts 18:11). Paul left Corinth for Ephesus, journeyed to
Jerusalem, visited other points in this area, passed through the "upper
country," and returned again to Ephesus (Acts 18:19–19:1). Barrett dates
his return to Ephesus as occurring in the late summer of A.D. 52.[3] The
Pentecost that he wanted to spend in Jerusalem (Acts 20:16) could have
been that of A.D. 55 (Acts 19:10; 20:31). The Pentecost of 1 Corinthians
16:8 could be that of either A.D. 53 or 54. The letter could have been sent
from Ephesus in either of these years.

The Importance of 1 Corinthians

Theologically Paul presents many vital truths in 1 Corinthians. Christ is
discussed as the wisdom of God (chs. 1 and 2), the second Adam (15:22),
and the agent in creation (8:6). The centrality of the crucifixion of Christ is
thoroughly explained in 1:18–2:5. The importance of the Resurrection is
underscored in 15:1–58. The role of the Holy Spirit in the production of
spiritual gifts is discussed at length in chapters 12–14. The nature of the
church as a holy and redemptive body is clarified by Paul's discussion of
church discipline in chapter 5. The unity and interdependence of the
body of Christ are portrayed in 12:4–27.

Practically, this letter shows the personal character of Paul as a pastor
and counselor. It demonstrates his wisdom, earnestness, and compassion
for his converts. It projects the principles that Paul used in the conflict of
Christianity with paganism in such matters as individual purity, social
relations, and family problems. In 6:1–8 Paul deals with the practical
problem that led Christians to go to court against other Christians. In
8:1–11:1 Paul confronted the problem that many people had of eating
meat that had been offered to idols and attendance at pagan temple feasts.

---

[2]For a discussion of the inscriptions see C. K. Barrett, *The New Testament Background*
(New York: Harper & Row, 1961), pp. 48–49.

[3]C. K. Barrett, *A Commentary on the First Epistle to the Corinthians*, 2nd ed., Black's
New Testament Commentaries (London: Adam and Charles Black, 1971), p. 5.

Here Paul urges his readers to be concerned with less stable brethren, and he proclaims that sacrificial love is more important than knowledge and privileges. In 7:1–40 Paul deals with the questions of marriage, divorce, celibacy, and widows.

This epistle allows us to see Paul not as an ivory-tower theologian but as an intensely concerned pastor striving for the holiness and maturity of his flock. He clearly articulates Christian doctrinal responses to pagan perversions and corruptions of the truth. Churches today can profit from the insight, wisdom, devotion, and challenge of Paul's words.

Outline

I. Paul and His Readers (1 Cor. 1:1–9)
  A. Salutation (1:1–3)
    1. Writer (1:1)
    2. Recipients (1:2)
    3. Greetings (1:3)
  B. Thanksgiving (1:4–9)
    1. Gratitude for God's grace (1:4–6)
    2. Results from God's grace (1:7–8)
    3. The dependability of God's grace (1:9)
II. Factions in the Church (1 Cor. 1:10–4:21)
  A. An Appeal for Unity (1:10)
  B. A Statement of the Facts (1:11–17)
    1. The source of Paul's information (1:11)
    2. The nature of the factions (1:12)
    3. A denial by Paul that he in any way encouraged this (1:13–17)
  C. Reasons for Factions (1:18–4:13)
    1. Misunderstanding of the Christian message (1:18–3:4)
      a) The gospel as God's saving power (1:18–2:5)
      b) The gospel as divine wisdom (2:6–3:4)
    2. False conception of the Christian ministry (3:5–4:5)
    3. Human pride (4:6–13)
  D. Appeal for Reconciliation (4:14–21)
III. Moral Problems (1 Cor. 5:1–6:20)
  A. Incest (5:1–13)
    1. Facts of the case (5:1–2)
    2. Action to be taken (5:3–8)
    3. Explanation (5:9–13)
  B. Dealings With Heathen Courts (6:1–11)
    1. A rebuke (6:1–8)

Chapter 1

Paul and His Readers
(1 Corinthians 1:1–9)

Paul's opening words to the church at Corinth follow a common first-century pattern in which the writer used the formula: A to B, greetings! Paul's words contain certain specifically Christian greetings and ideas not found in contemporary secular letters.

Later Paul will severely criticize his readers. Here he offers praise for the grace of God that has transformed their lives and has provided them spiritual gifts for building up the church, a theme to be discussed later in the book (chs. 12–14).

A. Salutation (1:1–3)

1. *Writer* (1:1)

Paul identifies himself to the Corinthians, notes his call to be an apostle, and recognizes that this call is due to the will of God. He is careful to state that he had not assumed office on his own initiative. "All the providential circumstances of Paul's birth and education, whereby his apostolic mission had been prepared for" are seen as a part of the will of God (Godet).

Sosthenes may refer to the former synagogue leader, now a brother in Christ (Acts 18:17). If this Sosthenes is the same as the synagogue leader of Acts, he had migrated to Ephesus from Corinth. Godet sees Sosthenes as Paul's secretary, who shared to an extent in the composition of 1 Corinthians. The mention of his name suggests that he enjoyed a high consideration among the Corinthians and may have cooperated with Paul in the evangelization of Corinth and Achaia.

2. *Recipients* (1:2)

The Christians at Corinth are described first as the "church of God," the term used by Paul to refer to the church in a specific location, and it refers to all believers in Christ in Corinth.

They are also designated as those who are "sanctified in Christ Jesus."
Goodspeed describes the Corinthians as "those who are consecrated by
union with Christ Jesus." Later Paul will soundly rebuke the Corinthians
for their sins, but here he forcefully asserts their sanctity. When the
Corinthians embraced Christ by faith, they were "transplanted from the
soil of our natural and profane life into that of his *Divine* holiness" (Godet). This description designates the spiritual potential of the position in
which they were living.

The Corinthians are called to be saints, along with those in every
location who call on the name of Jesus Christ as Lord. The phrase "with
all . . . who call . . . ," modifies "called." God calls His people from
every location, and all of His people acknowledge Christ as common
Lord.

3. *Greetings* (1:3)

Paul's greeting here is characteristic of his greetings in his other letters
(Rom. 1:7; 2 Cor. 1:2; Gal. 1:3). Grace is that act of God which serves as
the "ground of all Christian existence" (Barrett). Peace "is not simply the
absence of strife, but the presence of positive blessings. It is the prosperity of the whole man, especially his spiritual prosperity" (Morris).
These words by Paul are actually a prayer in which he urges the Corinthians to look again to the Father and the Son as the sources of full salvation.

B. Thanksgiving (1:4–9)

Galatians is the sole letter of Paul in which he passes immediately from
his greeting to his subject without expressing thanksgiving. Paul's intense
feelings about the apparent defection of the Galatians led him to make
this omission. In 1 Corinthians and in other letters he expresses gratitude
for what God has previously done, and he states a desire for further
progress. His words doubtless earned the good will of the Corinthians,
but he is not merely making a clever ploy to earn their attention. Neither
is he resorting to irony. His thanksgiving is spoken in full earnest, for he is
genuinely thankful for God's grace in their lives.

1. *Gratitude for God's grace* (1:4–6)

Although there were many problems in the lives of the Corinthians,
there must have been a contrast between their lives and that of the
heathen in Corinth (6:11). Paul's gratitude is directed to God and is not
addressed as a mere commendation to the Corinthians. The grace of God
is the source of all their spiritual blessings and includes their entire

experience of salvation. It is thus a general term and should not be limited merely to the spiritual gifts that Paul will discuss later.

In verse 5 Paul thanks God for two gifts that are highly prized by the Greeks. These are speaking, the proclamation of truth, and knowledge, the grasp of truth. Moffatt renders the verse: "In him you have received a wealth of all blessing, full power to speak of your faith, and full insight into its meaning."

The Corinthians placed great emphasis on the rhetorical ability of the speaker, but Paul is not commending mere rhetoric here. Elsewhere he notes that the power of his message was based on his deep conviction and dependence on divine resources (1:18; 2:4; 4:20). Bruce notes that the Corinthians "prized knowledge because they believed it gave them access to the divine mysteries . . . , but it probably did not have for them the more technical sense of *gnosis* associated with the developed Gnosticism of the following century."

Paul states in verse 6 that "the changed lives of the Corinthians demonstrated conclusively the validity of the message that had been preached to them" (Morris).

2. Results from God's grace (1:7–8)

The term "gift" in verse 7 can be used of salvation viewed as a gift (Rom. 5:15), God's gifts in general (Rom. 11:29), or of the gifts of the Spirit (12:4). The expressions "speaking" and "knowledge" in verse 5 would suggest that the reference to "gifts" is describing "the new spiritual powers with which the Spirit had endowed the members of the Church at Corinth" (Godet). This present taste of the Spirit turned the thoughts of the Corinthians to those fuller experiences to be granted on the occasion of the return of Christ (Eph. 1:13,14).

The term "blameless" in verse 8 suggests that the Christian is exempt from accusation. In the day of final judgment no charge can be placed against those who are declared safe through Christ (Rom. 8:33). J. B. Phillips renders the verse: "He will keep you steadfast in the faith to the end, so that when his day comes you need fear no condemnation."

3. The dependability of God's grace (1:9)

The character of God guarantees the acceptance of the believer on the day of Christ. Despite man's unfaithfulness God Himself is faithful. Christians have a share in a fellowship with Christ, and they share in the position of the exalted Lord.

For Further Study

1. Read articles on "Corinth" and on the Corinthian Epistles in *The Zondervan Pictorial Encyclopedia of the Bible*.

2. Read the letter of 1 Corinthians at least one time in a modern translation. Note repeated words, phrases, and themes. In a second or later reading make a personal outline of the letter.

Chapter 2

Factions in the Church
(1 Corinthians 1:10–4:21)

Paul begins this section of his letter with an appeal for unity. He defends his appeal with a statement of the fact prompting it. Paul had learned that cliques had developed among the Corinthians because they championed various human leaders. In verse 13 he notes the foolishness of such following after merely human leaders, and in verses 14–17 he indicates that he had done nothing to encourage partisanship after him.

Paul attributes the presence of these cliques to three sources. In 1:18–3:4 he warns the Corinthians that they had substituted worldly wisdom for divine wisdom. They gloried in the form of the message and in the messenger rather than receiving humbly the contents of the message. In 3:5–4:5 he indicates that they had looked on ministers such as himself and Apollos as competitors rather than as fellow workers with God. He warns them that they could destroy God's church by partisan following of human leaders, and he urges the Corinthians to withhold final judgment of the work of a minister. They must leave that task to God. In 4:6–13 he blames the human pride of the Corinthians as the culprit for much of their spiritual difficulty. In 4:14–21 Paul admonishes the Corinthians to unity in light of their relation to him as spiritual father.

A. An Appeal for Unity (1:10)

The apostles called on the name of Jesus for healing (Acts 3:6), baptizing (Acts 2:38), and in pronouncing judgment (5:4). Here the name of Jesus is invoked to heal the wounds threatening to divide a church. Paul makes his appeal on the basis of the spiritual kinship existing between him and the Corinthians.

His appeal that they might say the same things is seen by Barrett as a call for peaceful coexistence. The term "divisions" is a reference to differences of opinion that can lead to sin and contentious rivalry. The Greek word translated "perfectly united" is used in Matthew 4:21 to describe the mending of nets. Paul is asking the Corinthians to mend their differences and to come to a united outlook. Godet notes that the term "mind" described "the Christian way of thinking in general," and he feels that "thought" denotes the "manner of deciding a particular point." What Paul thus wants is a full harmony of view with regard to Christian truth and an agreement in the manner of settling specific questions. Bruce notes that the divisions had not yet developed, but if the quarrelings continued unchecked, outright division would result.

B. A Statement of the Facts (1:11–17)

In describing to the Corinthians what he knows of their dissensions Paul first indicates that he speaks with authoritative knowledge. He also indicates in some detail what he knows about the nature of the divisions. He wants the Corinthians to be surprised at his knowledge of their problem. He further wants to make it clear that he has not encouraged the present factions. He did not baptize for the purpose of building personal allegiance.

1. *The source of Paul's information* (1:11)

Paul reports the facts so that there can be no question as to his knowledge. The identity of Chloe is not certain, but she was likely a woman of some wealth with Christian servants who had recently visited Paul or had sent him a letter outlining the difficulties in the church. Both Robertson and Plummer feel that Chloe was an Ephesian woman with some Christian slaves who had visited Corinth and then reported back to Paul. She may not have been a Christian, but she seems to have been known to the Christians.

The report from Chloe's people indicates that there were contentions among the Corinthians. These were bitter discussions that could easily develop into splits or schisms. The differences among the Corinthians had led to quarrels in which everyone held his own opinion or view as correct and detested the views of others.

2. *The nature of the factions* (1:12)

The dissension that Paul now addresses may have been due to doctrine, personality, or some combination of both. Nothing in the passage suggests that the persons named were responsible for the discord that was present.

The mere appearance of these parties distressed Paul, and he professes no pleasure even in the group that claims him as their leader. The differences existing between the groups that championed Paul and Apollos were not doctrinal, but they revolved around different ways of stating the same truths. Paul had a rough and simple eloquence, and Apollos had a more elaborate and refined eloquence. Apollos' methods would more naturally appeal to the intellect of the Corinthians, but we read in 3:6–9 that Paul does not even hint that there are any differences between them. Peter's membership among the Twelve would give him authority, but he may never have visited Corinth. Bruce feels that this group represented a judaizing tendency that did not insist on circumcision but that did insist on the food restrictions imposed on gentile Christians by the Jerusalem decree of Acts 15:28,29.

The slogan "I follow Christ" may be Paul's personal answer to the other slogans, or it might refer to a prideful group claiming spiritual superiority. Bruce feels that this group refers to some self-styled "spiritual men" who defined God in terms of philosophical monotheism, defined freedom in terms of freedom from the rigors of Palestinian practices of legalism, and defined immortality as sound Greek doctrine of soul immortality in contrast with the Jewish idea of the Resurrection.

Paul appreciated loyalty, but he would have nothing to do with the partisanship that was developing at Corinth. He saw it as glorying in human qualities instead of the marvelous display of God's wisdom.

3. *A denial by Paul that he in any way encouraged this* (1:13–17)

In the first question of verse 13 Paul indicated that the divisions at Corinth were improper and sinful because they attempted to fragment Christ. The inference from the terse question of Paul is that Christ is one, and He is not divided into fragments and distributed among different groups. Paul appeals to the person of God's Son by his use of the word "Christ," and he mentions His work in the word "crucified." These factors should unite believers and leave no room for attachment anywhere else.

In the last two questions of verse 13 Paul indicates that the divisions were improper and sinful because human leaders could never take the place of Christ. Grosheide indicates that "to be baptized into the name of someone means to be brought into the most intimate relation with this person's revelation." With horror Paul recoils from the suggestion that anyone has been brought into an intimate relation with him. It was Christ with whom they had become intimately related.

Paul's statements about baptism in verses 14–17 are not a denunciation of baptism. He is simply affirming that he did not practice it with the purpose of recruiting personal followers. Paul indicates that he will not preach with wisdom of words but with a trust in God's work through

Christ. He took great care that he might not rely on rhetoric or human persuasion lest his hearers forget the importance of the Christian message.

Christ seems to have delegated baptism to His followers (John 4:2). Peter may have done the same (Acts 10:48). Paul does not indicate here why he handled Crispus, Gaius, and Stephanas differently from others. Crispus is likely the synagogue ruler whose conversion is narrated in Acts 18:8. Gaius is probably Paul's host in Corinth mentioned in Romans 16:23. Stephanas is mentioned in 1 Corinthians 16:15,17.

Knox translates the phrase "words of human wisdom" by the vivid metaphor, "with an orator's cleverness." In this phrase Paul introduces the Greek concept of wisdom to which he now turns his attention in the succeeding section.

C. Reasons for Factions (1:18–4:13)

Paul has played the role of a competent internist in diagnosing the existence of a divisive illness in the Corinthian church. He now explains the causes of their sickness by referring to their improper grasp of the Christian message in 1:18–3:4. The Corinthians looked on the gospel as a human system of philosophy or wisdom and belittled the simple proclamation of the cross. They also had a false concept of the Christian ministry (3:5–4:5). They saw preachers as rival party leaders and emphasized the importance of the human element in the work of the gospel. In 4:6–13 Paul pointed to their human pride as the source of their problems.

1. Misunderstanding of the Christian message (1:18–3:4)

In showing that the Corinthians do not understand the Christian message Paul contrasts worldly wisdom with divine wisdom. In 1:18–2:5 he indicates that the world regards God's wisdom as foolishness. Paul indicates that God has defeated human wisdom by using the preaching of the gospel to present Christ as God's power and wisdom. God has further defeated human wisdom at Corinth (vv. 26–31) by working through the weak and despised people of the city rather than with the wise and powerful. Paul indicates in 2:1–5 that the message of the gospel in its ability to change men demonstrated the power of God's wisdom rather than man's wisdom.

In 2:6–16 Paul continues to contrast true wisdom with worldly wisdom. True wisdom has its source in God, not the rulers of this age (v. 6). True wisdom is revealed to man by the Spirit of God (vv. 10–12). It is communicated to other men by Spirit-taught believers who know how to combine spiritual truths with spiritual words (vv. 13–16). In 3:1–4 Paul indicates that their immaturity prevents them from receiving more advanced truth.

a) *The gospel as God's saving power* (1:18–2:5)

In verse 18 the "message of the cross" is a synonym for the gospel. The Corinthians regarded the Christian message as a human philosophy to be discussed. Paul saw the gospel as good news to be proclaimed and believed. He viewed the gospel as a divine remedy for sin, not a human philosophy or system for speculation. This simple proclamation of the cross, seen by the Corinthians as both folly and weakness, is truly the wisdom and power of God.

The preaching of the cross is not primarily an appeal to the reasoning part of man's nature. It is an appeal to something deeper within him—his will and his entire personality.

The phrases, "those who are perishing" and "us who are being saved," are both present participles "expressing two acts which are passing into fulfilment at the very time when Paul mentions them" (Godet). Paul is suggesting that the hearing of the gospel consummates perdition in some and salvation in others.

In verse 19 Paul refers to Isaiah 29:14 in order to prove what he has stated in verse 18. He indicates that worldly cleverness fails in dealing with the things of God. Isaiah sees the failure of worldly statesmanship in Judah in the face of the judgment of the Assyrian invasion. Paul takes this principle and applies it to the failure of worldly wisdom in the face of the cross.

Paul's use of the terms "wise man" and "scholar" in verse 20 may refer respectively to Greeks and Jews. The term "philosopher" may refer equally well to both Greeks and Jews. The three terms describe those who are wise and learned as the world counts wisdom. Paul's statement is an echo of the words of Isaiah 33:18, where the collapse of Assyrian plans against Jerusalem is celebrated. God has not merely disregarded the wisdom of the world, but He has made it foolish. He had shown the futility of the world's wisdom by allowing it to effect its own results and by accomplishing with the cross what human wisdom could never perform (Robertson and Plummer). Phillips asks the question, "Has not God made the wisdom of this world look foolish?"

In verse 21 Paul uses two references to "wisdom." The first is a reference to the wisdom of God, the scheme or plan of God prepared and enacted for man's salvation. The second reference is a description of man's wisdom in its own efforts to know and reach God. The message that God saved men through a crucified Savior was not foolish, but to men it appeared as foolish. In this situation the world's wisdom failed, and the divine foolishness or wisdom succeeded. "What was preached" is not a mere reference to the act of preaching, but it stands for the gospel or the word of the cross. The entire phrase, "foolishness of what was preached," is a figure of speech known as an oxymoron, a combination of words whose contrasting meanings make the expression more vivid by appearing to contradict in a rather ludicrous way. Bruce notes that "Greek wisdom and philosophy . . . had neither led men to the knowledge of God nor brought them deliverance from sin; but these ends had now been achieved by the folly of the *kērygma*."

In verses 22–25 Paul indicates that Christ has become God's power and wisdom among those Jews and Greeks who are saved. Paul divides the world into two classes of men. The Jews have been enlightened by a special revelation from God, and they demand that God produce evidences of His existence as seen in external signs or visible demonstrations of power. Such a demand was a refusal to take God on trust, for it called on Him to present His credentials in a visible, identifiable act (Barrett). A crucified Messiah was unthinkable to the Jews (Deut. 21:23; Gal. 3:13), and they saw the cross as a refutation of Christ's claims. The Greeks attempted to reason their way to God by human speculation. For God to take a human form and die was incomprehensible to them.

For those Greeks and Jews who are called as heirs of salvation, Christ becomes the power of God to overcome sin and the wisdom of God who provides the method for their salvation. To describe believers as the "called" suggests that salvation "is rooted ultimately in a divine, not a human decision" (Barrett).

In verse 25 Paul indicates that the apparent weakness of God in allowing His Son to hang on the cross is stronger and more effective than any human effort (Hillyer). What God has done through the crucified Savior appears to be a direct contradiction of the human ideas of power and accomplishment. However, it has achieved what human wisdom has not accomplished—the release of man from bondage.

The words of Paul should not be mistakenly understood as looking with disdain on any attempt to make the form of one's preaching or teaching attractive, logical, and well-structured. They are intended to warn the person who relies largely on form that the unadorned, simple message of the gospel is sufficient to save men. It is the content of the message and not its form alone that provides power.

Barker, Lane, and Michaels suggest that the Corinthians had been influenced in their view of teaching style by a group of itinerant teachers known as Sophists (pp. 167,168). These Sophists used a particular style of teaching, were eloquent in their oratorical presentations, and were popular debaters. Paul's terms in 1:20 and 21 for "wise man," "philosopher of this age," and "wisdom of the world" are seen as technical terms familiar to the vocabulary of the Sophists. Perhaps some of these Sophists had made their way to Corinth and had shaped the expectations of the Corinthians concerning preaching and teaching style. The result was that Paul's simple, unadorned statement of the gospel didn't impress them as eloquent or appealing.

The evidence is that Paul's argument for a simple but forceful statement of the gospel became the message of early Christians. The declaration of Christ's life, death, burial, and resurrection (15:1–11) became the means of bringing the power of God into countless lives in the New Testament world.

In verses 26–31 Paul calls attention to the composition of the Corinthian church. In this section he stresses the sovereignty of God's working in the plan of salvation. In verse 27 Paul twice uses the word "chose," a term frequently used in the New Testament to express the choice of God in salvation (Acts 15:7; Eph. 1:4). He also emphasizes the unpromising backgrounds of those Corinthians whom God had chosen.

In verse 26 Paul shows the paradox of God's method among the socially despised membership in Corinth. He indicates that few who were wise by human standards were in the membership at Corinth. Phillips renders the latter part of verse 26 by saying that the Corinthian church did not consist of "many of the ruling class, nor many from the noblest families." The "calling" of the Corinthians was their divine call to salvation, not to a vocation in the present sense of the term. Some of the converts at Corinth such as Erastus (Rom. 16:23) may have been men of rank, but most of the Corinthians were either slaves or freedmen.

An interesting comment on Paul's description of the church at Corinth is provided by the pagan opponent of Christianity, Celsus, who denounced the Christian appeal to the lower classes with the words:

> The following are the rules laid down by them. Let no one come to us who has been instructed, or who is wise or prudent (for such qualifications are deemed evil by us); but if there be any ignorant, or unintelligent, or uninstructed, or foolish persons, let them come with confidence. By which words, acknowledging that such individuals are worthy of their God, they manifestly show that they desire and are able to gain over only the silly, and the mean, and the stupid, with women and children.—Origen, *Against Celsus*, 3:44

In verses 27 and 28 Paul indicates that God has chosen those things that are foolish and weak in order to shame those things that are wise and strong. It was not that God had selected those who were merely viewed as foolish and weak—they really were. The term "base" (KJV) in verse 28 means low-born, sometimes morally worthless. The description of the moral background of the Corinthians in 6:9–11 shows that God took some who were morally worthless and made them into a church. The word "nullify" in verse 28 means to render ineffective or worthless. The NEB suggests that by using people of humble and despised background God has overthrown "the existing order." Barrett notes, "When God set his plan in motion there was no church in Corinth, save in his intention; notwithstanding opposition (and in its own weakness), it now existed."

Paul indicates in verse 29 that God has done all this with the purpose of taking away from men any opportunity for personal boasting. Christians were actually glorying in men! Paul wanted them to know that their spiritual existence was dependent on the call of God and that their message was the preaching of the cross. Christians were not to boast in merely human instruments.

In verses 30 and 31 Paul again reminds the Corinthians that the gospel is a message designed to enhance the glory of God. All spiritual possessions are due to Him alone. Paul begins verse 30 with a reminder that God is the source of the new spiritual life available in Christ Jesus. Williams puts it graphically when he says, "So you owe it all to him through union with Christ Jesus." The terms "righteousness," "holiness," and "redemption" denote aspects of the wisdom that believers find in Christ (Bruce). Morris notes that "*righteousness* in this context will stand for that righteousness which Christ makes available for men." Holiness is progress toward perfect holiness, and redemption may point "to the last great day, the consummation of redemption" (Morris). This final redemption is possible because Christ has paid the ransom price in His death at Calvary. Paul's final words in verse 31 remind men that they cannot boast of themselves, but they can boast in Christ through whom they have all things. The words resemble Jeremiah 9:23 and 24, but they are a free quotation. In the original context the words refer to Jehovah, and their use here portrays a high view of the person of Christ. Words applied to the eternal God in the Old Testament are here seen as referring to His Son Jesus Christ.

In 2:1–5 Paul describes the message, manner, and motive of his preaching at the time of the establishment of the Corinthian church. He was seeking to demonstrate that the salvation of the Corinthians had come through the message of the cross and not through human wisdom. The message of Paul was the simple declaration of the death of Jesus Christ. His manner was to proceed with an anxious desire to accomplish God's task. His motive was to ground the faith of his audience in the power of God and not in human wisdom.

Paul's statements concerning his message in verses 1 and 2 bear witness to the work of God in Christ for men's salvation. Because Paul's preaching was so simple and unpretentious, its astounding results demonstrated convincingly the power of God. The emphatic words "When I," beginning verse 1, indicate that Paul was a living example of the truth of divine power that he expounded. He claimed no superiority for "his speech, the way in which he presented his facts, or for his wisdom, the way in which his mind marshalled his facts" (Morris). Paul was asserting that he did not proclaim the gospel with great oratorical talent. Some manuscripts include the word "mystery" in verse 1 instead of "testimony." The former reading would be in line with 2:7, and the latter reading with 1:6. "The gospel was both the message to which the apostles bore witness and the divine revelation, previously concealed, which they made known" (Bruce). Knox emphasizes that in verse 1 Paul indicated that he came "without any high pretensions to eloquence, or to philosophy."

Some feel that Paul's statement of his message in verse 2 reflects a change on his part adopted because of his poor success at Athens (Acts 17:22–31). Against this interpretation is his comment in Galatians 3:1, which indicates that his policy in Corinth and among the Galatians was the same. The reference to "Jesus Christ and him crucified" indicates that the person and work of Jesus the Messiah comprises the entire gospel. For Paul this message would include the Resurrection as well as the Crucifixion (15:1–11).

The words of verse 3 describe the manner of Paul in his work among the Corinthians. Robertson and Plummer suggest that Paul's weakness here may have been due to a combination of his unimpressive presence (2 Cor. 10:10), his shyness in venturing unaccompanied into strange surroundings (Acts 17:15; 18:5), his poor success at Athens, the wickedness of Corinth, and the potential hostility of the Jews (Acts 18:5–6). In addition he may have had a physical malady that first hindered his preaching at Galatia (Gal. 4:13). This may have been his thorn in the flesh (2 Cor. 12:7). The words "fear" and "trembling" are not seen as due to personal danger but stem from a "trembling desire to perform a duty" (Robertson and Plummer). Bruce sees the overall emphasis as referring more "to a sense of complete personal inadequacy in view of the task of evangelizing such a city as Corinth." The haughty Corinthians are told that Paul could not perform his work in Corinth from a spirit of self-sufficiency but he was humbly dependent on the power of the indwelling Christ.

The motive of Paul's preaching is elaborated in verses 4 and 5. In verse 4 the term "message" is a reference to the gospel, the contents of Paul's message. The term "preaching" portrays the act of proclamation. Here Paul specifically disclaimed the cleverness of the rhetorician. His manner was plain and lacking in flights of oratory or philosophy. Paul denounces "persuasive words," words calculated to be enticing by human standards. In the word translated "demonstration" the "premises are known to be true, and therefore the conclusion is not only logical, but certainly true"

(Robertson and Plummer). Paul is here not dealing with scientific certainty, but he suggests that the certitude of religious truth for the believer is as complete and as objective as the certainty of scientific truth for the scientific mind. The two proofs will differ in kind, but are the same in degree. Paul suggests that even his rhetorical defects did not hinder a convincing demonstration of the power of the Spirit. Whenever he preached, a divine power gripped his hearers and drove them to repentance and faith (Barrett).

Paul's motive is stated even more clearly in verse 5. Here it is indicated that he sought to assure that the faith of the Corinthians was divinely based and was not due to human persuasion. Preaching that depended on human logic and rhetoric for its effect could only produce a faith that was dependent on the same props. Such a faith could vanish in the face of flowery logic and oratory. Paul would have none of this. He dreaded "giving rise to cases of adherence which would have rested only on an intellectual or aesthetical, and consequently superficial, attraction" (Godet). Paul did commend Christ to the attention of the wise, but he always maintained the statement of the simple gospel of the crucified Savior. Even in Athens (Acts 17:22–31), although his approach was made through the use of the culture of Athens, he concluded with a reference to the gospel as seen in the Resurrection of Christ.

Nothing in Paul's words should be seen as an invitation to the contemporary preacher to make his words dull and insipid. God's message is to be presented in a creative, arresting manner. The gospel must also be plain, clear, and undiluted. Paul feared greatly the dilution of the gospel by an excessive emphasis on form. So long as the content of the gospel is kept intact, the method of presenting it may be adjusted to the audience.

b) *The gospel as divine wisdom* (2:6–3:4)

Here Paul asserts that there is true wisdom in the gospel, but it is understood only by the mature. In these verses there is a description of the wisdom of the gospel not as the wisdom of the world but as the wisdom of God (v. 6). The wisdom of the world is marked by rebellion against God. The divine wisdom is characterized as a wisdom hidden in a mystery (vv. 7–9). The source of this revealed wisdom is indicated in 2:10–16 as the Spirit of God. The recipients of this wisdom are described in 3:1–4. Notice the three classes of people as indicated by the terms "without the Spirit," ("natural," KJV), "spiritual," and "carnal" or "worldly" appearing in 2:14–3:4. The interpretation of these terms will be important in deciphering Paul's meaning.

In this section Paul uses the term "wisdom" in both a bad and a good sense. It is used in a bad sense "when it denotes simply the skilled marshalling of human arguments, employed with a view to convincing the hearer" (Barrett). This process becomes evil when it veils the power of the Spirit by a demonstration of human cleverness. It can lead to a position in which wisdom is evaluated by human and not by divine standards. In a good sense "wisdom" may refer to "God's wise plan of redeeming the world through a crucified Messiah," and it may be used to denote "the actual substance of salvation itself as given through the wise plan of salvation" (Barrett).

In 2:6 Paul indicates to the Corinthians that he cannot talk to them about the wisdom of God, for they are infants. They are not sufficiently mature to grasp what he is saying. In speaking of the Corinthians as immature, Paul is not using gnostic terms to distinguish between earthly and spiritual men. There are different classes among Christians, but there is no gradation of caste. All Christians have equal access to the wisdom of God, and they must be trained to receive it.

Paul's use of the term "rulers of this age" is seen by some as a reference to demons. Some feel that Paul envisages Christ as engaged in a titanic struggle with the forces of the unseen world. Against this interpretation is the recognition that throughout this passage Paul's contrast is between the wisdom of God as shown in the gospel and the wisdom of men. It would be an extraneous concept now to introduce the thought of the wisdom of demonic powers. Also, in verse 8 Paul identifies the rulers of the world as those who crucified Christ in ignorance. The most likely understanding of the term is of the Jewish and Roman leaders who crucified Christ.

Paul indicates that these rulers are doomed to pass away. They are on the way out because Christ is now reigning (15:25) and their authority is at an end (Col. 2:15).

In verses 7–9 Paul describes God's wisdom as "hidden," or as a mystery. The idea of mystery indicates a secret that man cannot penetrate but which God reveals. God's wisdom is hidden in that it has only been disclosed at the turning of the ages in the decisive appearance of Jesus Christ. Barrett notes that it may also be hidden in that it has nothing to do with persuasive words of human wisdom. Before time began, God was concerned for our glory, and He ordained through the gospel that human beings should enter into glory. The wisdom of God leads to glory inasmuch as it leads to obedience (Rom. 8:16,17). This glory awaits men in the age to come (15:43), but it also can be experienced in the present as people live out the power of the indwelling Spirit of God (2 Cor. 3:18). Williams graphically portrays this verse as speaking of "a wisdom that came from God, once a covered secret but now uncovered, which God marked off as His plan for bringing us to glory."

In verse 8 Paul indicates that the rulers of the time showed their lack of understanding in their treatment of Christ. He reasons that if the rulers of this world had grasped who Jesus was, they would never have rejected Him. The title for Jesus, "Lord of glory," also appears in James 2:1. Godet sums up the significance of these words when he says:

> If the representatives of Jewish wisdom and Roman power had understood the higher glory which Jesus was bringing to them, they would undoubtedly have sacrificed that which they possessed. But as they did not discern the former, they chose at any price to maintain their earthly power, and they sought to destroy Him at whose feet they should have abdicated.

In verse 9 Paul makes a free citation of Isaiah 64:4 with verbal parallels to Isaiah 65:17 and 52:15. In His wisdom God has prepared for His own people such good things as the mind of man cannot conceive. The dominant thought here is a reference to those things that God gives to His people in the final blessed consummation, but there is also some reference to the present blessings that God gives to His people. The heart of man in a biblical sense is the whole of his inner life including thought, will, and emotions. There is no method by which human organs can perceive the wonderful things that God has made ready for those who love Him.

Having stated the inability of man to plumb the greatness of God's gifts, Paul now suggests the source of comprehending the things of God (vv. 10–16). He first states that these "deep things of God" are made known through the Holy Spirit. The term "search" suggests "to penetrate." The "deep things of God" would be a reference to the innermost recesses of divine counsel. To these recesses the Spirit has access, and He lays bare their content to the believer. The words of Paul at this point resemble the emphasis in John 14:26 where the Spirit is described as the one who will "remind you of everything." There the emphasis is on aiding the disciples in recalling the teachings of Jesus. Here the promise is more fully related to giving spiritual insight into that which has not previously been spoken to man. Such knowledge as Paul describes is available to all believers, not simply to an inner ring of elect initiates.

In introducing verse 11 with "for" Paul is enlarging on the work of the Holy Spirit in revealing the things of God. Just as the human spirit can penetrate secrets of human self-consciousness, the Spirit of God has known God from within. An interesting by-product of Paul's statements in this verse is the bestowal of full divinity on the Holy Spirit.

In verse 12 the Spirit of God is contrasted with the spirit of the world which has the power to make revelations of another nature. This spirit is not a reference to the devil, but to a "man-centered planning in which man provides for his own interests, a condition in which it is impossible for him to understand the sort of divine truth that is manifested in Christ crucified" (Barrett). In briefer words it might be seen as the spirit of human wisdom or the temper of this world. This Holy Spirit is received at conversion (12:13) and constitutes the down payment of all the good things that God intends to do for His people (Eph. 1:13,14). The last clause of verse 12 indicates the purpose for receiving the Holy Spirit, "that we might get insight into the blessings God has graciously given us" (Williams). Paul makes no effort to define what these blessings are, and we are left with the same undefinable benefit as is mentioned in verse 9. They would seem to be qualities that are appropriate "to the life of heaven, but already freely given to Christians" (Barrett). Paul's descriptions of the "blessings in heavenly places" in Ephesians 1:3–14 refers to some of these blessings.

Paul follows his description of blessings freely bestowed on Christians with the statement that the Spirit provides language that makes conversation about the truths possible. The previous statements in verse 12 had more to do with revelation, God's communicating Himself to man. The statements of verse 13 refer to truth communicated from man to man. "The same Divine breath which lifted the veil *to reveal*, takes possession also of the mouth of its interpreter when it is *to speak*" (Godet). The communication of this truth is not inspired from secular wisdom but from the Spirit of God.

The latter section of verse 13 has been given various interpretations. The question revolves around whether the words for "spiritual" are to be taken to refer to persons or to content. The translations reflect this difficulty. The ASV suggests that the meaning is "combining spiritual things with spiritual words." Conybeare sees it as referring to "explaining spiritual things to spiritual men." The verb "combining" is given the meaning of "matching." Most modern commentators incline to the view that Paul speaks of combining spiritual things, the words spoken, with spiritual things, the truths expressed. They also normally agree with the assessment of Morris that "the solution is not easy, and a final decision perhaps impossible."

Paul's words in verses 14–16 continue to emphasize that the Holy Spirit is the source of spiritual insight. In verse 14 Paul uses the phrase "the man without the Spirit" ("natural," KJV) to refer to one who has not received the Holy Spirit and who is thus not a Christian. The term is sometimes rendered "soulish," and it refers to the "man whose horizon is bounded by the things of this life. It is the worldly-wise man again, the man who has been so much in Paul's thoughts throughout this passage" (Morris). Bruce points out that Adam was created "a living soul" and that the word used for soul comes from the same word family as the adjective for "natural" or "soulish." He concludes that "everything that belongs to our heritage from the first Adam, the father of our mortal humanity, is therefore *psychikon* [natural]; everything which we derive from union with the exalted Christ, the head of the new creation, is *pneumatikon* [spiritual], the more so as it is conveyed to us by the Spirit." The verb "judged" was used in a legal sense of the preliminary examination prior to the main hearing (Morris). It came to refer to scrutinizing, examining, or estimating. "Paul is insisting that the man whose equipment is only of this world, the man who has not received the Holy Spirit of God, has not the ability to make an estimate of things spiritual" (Morris).

By way of contrast, Paul mentions in verse 15 that the spiritual man accurately discerns or evaluates all things, both secular and spiritual. Because he has received the Spirit, he is able to appraise all things, for he both understands them and is furnished with a moral standard for proper measurement of them. Yet, this same spiritual man cannot be judged by the natural man. Bruce feels that Paul is asserting that "ultimately the man of God is answerable to God alone, and in any case he cannot be assessed at all by those who have not the same Spirit as he has received." Morris feels that it presents the spiritual man as "an enigma to the natural man. Because the natural man cannot know spiritual things (v. 14), he cannot judge the spiritual man."

In verse 16 Paul introduces a quote from Isaiah 40:13. The reference is intended to bolster his statement in verse 15 that only the spiritual man can properly evaluate the things of God. The Christian who is equipped with the mind of Christ possesses the equipment for deciphering the mind of the Lord. The Holy Spirit becomes the agent through whom this mind of God is made available to the spiritual man. The press agent of a politician will hold many conversations with his employer so that he may properly represent the politician's mind in a public forum. After an intimate discussion with the politician, he may properly say, "I have my employer's mind." The Christian is in a similar position in his position as to the insights and views of Christ.

In 3:1-4 Paul asserts that the immaturity of the Corinthians hinders their receiving fully the teaching he wants to give them. It is important at this point to contrast the manner in which Paul uses the terms "spiritual" and "worldly" appearing in 3:1-4 and his discussion of the natural man in 2:14. The natural man is one who lacks the Spirit of God. He is unregenerate, unconverted. The spiritual man is one who has the Spirit. He has access to the "deep things of God." In its meaning the term "spiritual" does not signify a believer who is spiritually advanced over other Christians. It refers simply to one who possesses the Spirit of God. It is Paul's assumption that this spiritual man will listen to the Spirit of God and learn the things of God, but the term here does not denote any elevated moral standard of commitment. The term "worldly" or "carnal" is denoted by two different but cognate terms in verse 1 and verse 3. The term in verse 1 is transliterated as *sarkinois*, and it refers to being made of flesh and blood. The term in verse 3 is transliterated as *sarkikoi*, and means to be characterized by flesh. Paul's reference in verse 1 is to the time when he first visited Corinth, and there would then be nothing wrong in saying that the young believers in Corinth were "made of flesh." They were young converts. They had had no time or opportunity for growth and could be expected to resemble their immature, fleshly background. For Paul to use the term "characterized by flesh" of those who had been Christians for some years was culpable. They should have progressed beyond spiritual infancy, and it was their fault that they had not.

In daily quality of Christian life the "natural" man, the man without the Spirit, likely resembles the "worldly" man quite closely. Both would have a preference for envy, strife, and jealousy, and could attach themselves to human leaders. The moral lifestyle of both would be accommodating and compromising. Paul uses the term "worldly" of an immature Christian who has the Holy Spirit, but who has not developed or matured in his spiritual life. Christians today must recognize that the person they regard as "worldly" may in reality be a "natural" man who has some of the outward trappings of Christianity. He may lack the presence of the Spirit of God, who alone can provide understanding of divine truth and progress in holiness.

In verse 1 Paul softens his words to the Corinthians by calling them "brothers." When Paul had been with them during his mission to Corinth, he could not address them as spiritual, for they were mere babes in Christ. They had just experienced regeneration. Paul attaches here no rebuke or shame to this position. These Corinthians were immature. Knox describes the Corinthians at this stage as "little children in Christ's nursery."

The spiritual food that Paul had given to the Corinthians was such as they could digest (v. 2). He describes this teaching as milk, and the same idea appears in Hebrews 5:11–14. There the term refers to elementary teaching. Grosheide sees it as "aimed especially at calling souls to surrender themselves to God; in other words: missionary preaching." He sees meat as "the symbol of a preaching to convinced Christians in which it is possible to unfold the full richness, the magnificence of the gospel." Paul finds them culpable because they had not grown with the passing of time.

The "for" of verse 3 explains the evidence of the carnality of these

Corinthians. The term "jealousy" refers to a zeal or ardor that can lead to envy. It is not a pejorative term in itself, but its presence can easily lead to "quarreling." The word for "quarreling" appeared in 1:11, and both words suggest self-assertion. The envy and strife were the opposite of the love that should characterize the Christian, and their presence indicates that the Corinthians were walking on a merely human level. They were attributing to men the traits and positions that properly belong only to God. Both words are included in the infamous list of the "works of the flesh" in Galatians 5:20.

Paul continues the explanation of his displeasure with the factions among the Corinthians in verse 4. The examples he uses, himself and Apollos, are selected to show that he does not blame anyone for hostility to him personally. He sees the mere presence of divisions as spiritually substandard. Here Paul uses only the partisans of himself and Apollos as examples, but it was from other parties that his chief troubles came. Apollos and his followers presented no challenge to the apostleship of Paul, but the attachment to either Paul or Apollos was a source of grief to the apostle. His complaint is that they were arguing exactly like worldly people, a totally un-Christian attitude. Each utterance of a party slogan, whether pro-Paul or pro-Apollos, showed that the Corinthians had merely worldly wisdom. In forgetting their dependence on God the Corinthians were showing themselves to be men and nothing more. Barrett tersely summarizes the attitude of Paul: "What is wrong is the resounding *ego* with which each slogan begins."

This verse leads naturally as a transition into the following passage. In order to attack the spirit of contention and the divisions in Corinth, Paul had spotlighted the false way in which the Corinthians had regarded the gospel. He viewed the preaching of the gospel not as the exposition of a new religious philosophy but as the simple statement of a fact, a fact viewed as absurd to the eyes of reason. From this he now proceeds to deduce the true role of the Christian ministry and its place within the church.

2. *False conception of the Christian ministry* (3:5–4:5)

The Corinthians saw preachers as leaders of rival parties and conflicting groups. They exaggerated the importance of the human element in the work of the gospel. Now Paul states his own view of the ministry as a corrective to the errors of the Corinthians. In 3:5–9 he indicates that ministers such as Apollos and himself are one in their purposes and are only servants of God. God Himself gives the increase. In 3:10–17 Paul points out his place in the life of the Corinthians and compares this to the role of others. He warns that the Corinthians must not allow partisanship to destroy God's temple. In 3:18–23 he warns the Corinthians that they must not glory in men, for through Christ all things belong to them. The ministry of the apostle is described as that of a servant of Christ and a steward of God's mysteries in 4:1–5. Paul indicates that only God can ultimately evaluate his motives and deeds.

Paul begins his question in verse 5 with a "what" and not a "who." This allows the Corinthians to concentrate on the functions of Paul and Apollos rather than on their persons. Paul's answer focuses on the unified purposes of both Apollos and himself. Both were servants of the one Lord and were themselves insignificant. The word "servants" was originally used of the service of a table waiter. It came to be used of service generally, and in the New Testament it often appears with the meaning of the service that one should give to God. It is not a high and lofty word. God had used the ministry of each apostle to evoke faith. To each man, Paul and Apollos, a different ministry had been given, but they were united as servants of the one Lord.

The agricultural symbols of verse 6 stress the limited character of Paul's work. Paul was the planter, the first evangelist. Apollos watered, as in Acts 18:27 and 28. The tenses used for "plant," "water," and "increase" present the thought that Paul and Apollos had done their work, but God's work was continuous. "The creation and nurturing of faith is the work neither of preacher nor of hearer, but of God" (Barrett). Williams renders this verse: "I did the planting, Apollos did the watering, but it was God who kept the plants growing."

Paul's conclusion in verse 7 is that neither the planter nor the waterer amount to anything. God is everything. The only significance of Paul and Apollos is that God accepted their works and worked through them. They have no independent importance. The attention of the Corinthians is to be fastened on God, not on His instruments. Williams says that "God is everything in keeping the plants growing." Godet notes that Paul directed verses 5–7 against the folly of raising servants to the rank of masters. The next verse compares Paul and Apollos with one another and contrasts them by noting their respective merits (Godet).

Paul notes the essential unity between planter and waterer (v. 8). They are one in the aim, result, and motivating power of their work. They are allies and not rivals. The fault of the Corinthians was their argument about which of the undergardeners was more significant. How foolish! Each laborer, however, has made his distinctive contributions, and each can expect his eventual reward for labor. The criterion of judgment will be labor and not success. Paul does not indicate whether this reward is heavenly or earthly, but Bruce interprets Paul's words by saying, "The planter and the waterer will be paid their appropriate wages on the 'day of

Christ'." Godet adds: "The estimate of the fidelity of each servant will not rest on the comparison of it with another's, but on the labour of each compared with his own task and his own gift. Now who else than God could pronounce such a sentence?"

In verse 9 Paul describes both himself and Apollos as God's fellow workers. Paul means either that they work together for God or work together with God. Since this context is discussing their position as servants, the former idea is preferable. Paul viewed the congregation as God's field, a cultivated piece of land now awaiting God's blessings. He also sees them as the building that God erected through His servants. The reference to "God" three times in this brief verse suggests the relative insignificance of human instruments. Paul uses the image of the building he has introduced as his basis for expressing the two different results that human labor may have.

In 3:10–17 Paul presents his role as that of a master builder, and he suggests how others can build on the foundation he has laid. The term "someone else" in verse 10 is primarily a reference to Apollos, but it also serves as a collective term and "denotes the whole body of individuals who, as prophets, teachers, . . . had laboured, since Paul's departure, in developing the Church founded by him" (Godet). Paul also introduces the image of a temple and warns the Corinthians against destroying this temple by partisan actions.

The term "expert builder" in verse 10 describes someone who superintends a building operation by contributing knowledge rather than labor. As a wise expert builder Paul had taken careful steps to avoid the development of factions. He refrained from divisive human speculation. The work that Paul accomplished was done in the strength of the grace of God, and there may be a particular reference to the work of Paul in founding new churches. The foundation laid is that of the proclamation of the gospel (v. 11). The structure built on it may refer either to doctrine or the body of Christ. Both may be partially in view. Although the primary emphasis of these verses applies to the work of teachers, it can also be taken as a warning to every believer to be careful how he or she builds on the foundation of Christ.

In verse 11 Paul emphasizes that men have no choice of foundation other than Jesus Christ in His person and work. Phillips says, "The foundation is laid already, and no one can lay another, for it is Jesus Christ himself." Historically, Paul is referring to the laying of the foundation in Christ when he preached the gospel in Corinth. It is possible that some from the party of Peter may have depreciated Paul's apostolic claims and may have reminded the Corinthians that it was to Peter that Jesus said,

"On this rock I will build my church" (Matt. 16:18). If that be true, Paul hastens to dispose of the idea by suggesting that only Christ provides an adequate foundation for the construction of the church of God.

The material that Paul describes in verse 12 can be divided into durable and perishable goods. The durable materials of gold, silver, and precious stones were used in the construction of ornate palaces and temples in Paul's lifetime. The reference to costly stones may refer to such costly building stones as granite or marble, which would be useful in ornamentation. The wood, hay, and straw would be used to construct many of the shacks sitting in the squalid slums of ancient cities. Paul's readers would be familiar with many instances in which fires broke out, spread rapidly throughout these cities, and consumed dwellings quickly. The likelihood of this tragedy in an ancient city would provide visible reminder to the Corinthians to build wisely on the foundation laid by Paul.

The day spoken of in verse 13 is the day when Christ returns and will institute judgment (1 Thess. 5:4). The judgment by fire will determine the quality of work. The "quality" of each person's work is emphasized rather than the quantity. The fire mentioned is not a retributive or punitive fire, but it is a fire of testing. The image is that of a fire which exposes materials of bad quality by reducing them to ashes while leaving the good materials intact. The work that is judged is more the work of an individual in building on the foundation rather than that of personal character.

A contrast between the work that remains and the work that is consumed is given in verses 14 and 15. There is a double result from the judgment of fire as mentioned in the preceding verse. By comparison with verse 15 it can be seen that the reward of verse 14 is not salvation itself. The distinction given here is between the saved who have built well and those who have built poorly. The parable of the pounds in Luke 19:11–27 suggests that the reward may consist of opportunities for higher service. The term "reward" would be better translated as "wage." Goodspeed renders the latter part of the verse as: "He will have his pay." The person whose reward disappears will be safe, but he will be like a man rescued from a fire. The image is that of a man who dashes through a fire to safety. "By the perishable *work* of this laborer, Paul understands the Christian life without seriousness, humility, self-denial, personal communion with Christ, which has been produced among the members of the Church by the ministry of a preacher solely concerned to move sensibility, to charm the mind and please his audience" (Godet). Such a teacher will receive no wages for his work. His loss is the loss of those wages, like a workman fined of his wages for poor work. Nevertheless this person shall be saved, for he has built on a proper foundation.

The concluding phrase of verse 15, "through the flames," is not a reference to the fires of hell. It is a reference to the fires of testing or judgment.

Paul's words have a blunt application to the minister or Christian worker of today who uses smooth, bland words to charm his people rather than to instill deep godliness in them. Such a person is more concerned for human approval and recognition than for divine acceptance. He may be a believer, but he need expect no reward for his unfaithful performance.

Paul's warning in verses 16 and 17 is to those people whose divisiveness threatened the very spiritual existence of the church at Corinth. In calling the church a temple Paul is speaking of the entire church and not merely teachers. Of two Greek words for temple Paul uses the word that referred to the shrine or sanctuary of the place of worship. He says that in believers the very presence of God exists. The Corinthians were made God's dwelling place by the presence of the Spirit of God. This the Corinthians had failed to grasp. The stern warning of verse 17 is addressed "to those who had laboured at Corinth in such a way that they had ended with disorganizing the Church, poisoning its religious and moral life, and compromising the Divine work so happily begun and carried forward in that great city" (Godet). The destruction that Paul threatens is not specified, but it refers to something grave. It represents some terrible ruin and eternal loss. Morris sees the person who is threatened as actually being unsaved.

The temple of God is holy in that it is set apart for God. The final sentence of the verse reminds the readers that in Christianity there is an individual and a corporate aspect.

Throughout much of chapter 2 Paul discusses the subject of worldly wisdom and its emptiness. He shows that the divisions among the Corinthians were based on their foolish attachment to worldly wisdom, and he moves to rebuke these divisions concerning personalities by affirming the lowly place these preachers have. In 3:18–23 he again treats the subject of worldly wisdom, and he reminds his readers that the wisdom of God is not to be evaluated by the rules of the philosophers.

Paul begins the section by calling on his readers to die to the wisdom of this world (v. 18). He first describes an individual who regards himself as wise in this present age. Such a person has assumed the pose of a wise man, the reputation of a profound thinker, and has taken up the philosophy of the world. Paul assures this person "that he will not attain to true wisdom till he has passed through a crisis in which that wisdom of his with which he is puffed up will perish" (Godet). Taylor paraphrases the verse as indicating that such a man should "be a fool rather than let it hold you back from the true wisdom from above." Paul then moves to justify the need for dying to the wisdom of the world.

He asserts that the worldly wisdom so highly valued by the Corinthians is unable to penetrate God's divine wisdom. In verse 19 Paul refers to Job 5:13 and uses the verse to show that the tricky measures of the wise become a net with which God captures them. They will ultimately be forced to concede that the wiser they have attempted to be, the more foolish they have actually become. "Catches" emphasizes that God has a strong grip on the slippery cleverness of the wicked. "Craftiness" stands for cunning, a readiness to do anything. The cunning of men is of no avail in the face of God's might and wisdom. In verse 20 Paul refers to Psalm 94:11. The "thoughts" to which he refers are plots or deliberate plans. Paul describes these plots as empty and ineffective in their very essence. God's plan of salvation is a thought of God that is superior to all the discoveries of human wisdom (2:6–8). The TCNT has rendered these words: "The Lord sees how fruitless are the deliberations of the wise." Man, who regards himself as wise, has not effected anything toward a lasting salvation. God, by the use of what men call foolishness, has set man free from sin, provided him with righteousness, and set him on the path to holiness.

In verse 21 Paul concludes his denunciation of the human wisdom that leads to division. Anyone who claimed only one of God's servants as a leader was demonstrating his enslavement to secular fads. By saying that "all things are yours" Paul meant that all the servants of God and their gifts of ministry were equally theirs. Paul's use of the term "all" is further detailed in the enumeration of verse 22. These misled Corinthians were cheating themselves by limiting themselves to only one of God's chosen people. Paul, Apollos, and Cephas are all the property of the congregation since God has put His servants at the disposal of the church. The church not only receives gifted men, but the world itself belongs to believers. Here the term "world" is not used in its ethical sense, but it refers to the entirety of creation seen as the proper inheritance for the Christian. The pair of experiences, "life" and "death," belong to the believer. Life in Christ, the only true life, is the possession of the Christian. Death, which includes all those forces that tend toward weakness, sickness, or decay, has been overcome by the Christian. From this pair of terms proceed many hostile influences affecting the believer, and in Christ he has triumphed over both. In relation to time the Christian can expect triumph in both the present and the future. By his use of the term "present" Paul includes all that can happen to us in our present state of living. In discussing "the future" he includes the eternal hopes and consequences that lie ahead. For the Christian all of these are equally in God's hands. This collection of terms resembles the catalog in Romans 8:35–39. Godet says that the purpose of Paul is "to exalt the consciousness of this Church, which is degrading itself by dependence on weak human instruments . . . , to the height of its glorious position in Christ. He strives to restore it to self-respect."

Paul completes his efforts to call the church to a proper view of its heritage in verse 23. To demolish the party spirit brewing among the Corinthians, he states that not one group of them, but all of them together, are Christ's. These words would be a particularly galling statement for the Christ party of 1:12. Not merely can a few self-righteous, pompous individuals claim that they are Christ's. This is the privilege of the entire church. Just as the church possesses all things because it depends on Christ, Christ possesses all things. His universal sovereignty rests on His full dependence in the Father (Phil. 2:5–11). A Christian cannot view the absolute dependence of the Son on the Father (Luke 22:42) and boast of himself or another. When a church and each individual Christian realize their immense privileges in Christ, the miserable selfishness among Christians can be banished.

Paul has spoken in this manner to make the Corinthians ashamed of their senseless infatuations. He now wants to wipe out the hasty judgments that some of the Corinthians harbor toward him. In 4:1–5 he moves to picture his position as that of a minister of Christ and a steward of God's hidden truths. Only the judgment of God concerning his own ministry is of concern to him.

Paul's words in verse 1 suggest a contrast with the heights to which he had raised his readers at the conclusion of 3:23. Paul suggests that the apostles are not competing party leaders but the humble servants of Christ. There are no lofty pretensions in Paul. The term for "servants" here is different from that used in 3:5. The term here was used outside the New Testament of an underrower, a servant who rowed in the lower bank of oars on a ship. Bruce feels that in practice there is little distinction in the words.

A steward had oversight of his master's household. The apostles, as God's stewards, were entrusted with the administration of the mysteries of God or the truths of the gospel. The NEB translates the first half of v. 1: "We must be regarded as Christ's underlings." Williams catches the thought of the final section with: "Trustees to handle God's uncovered truths."

The primary responsibility of a steward is that he be fully trustworthy (v. 2). By its very nature the work of a steward was not closely supervised. He was not to exercise his own personal authority and initiative, but he was expected to do his master's bidding. Before God a spiritual steward will be judged strictly on his faithfulness. It is at this point that the judgment of man is quite inadequate, and Paul now moves to make this clear.

In the previous verses the words related to preachers in general and especially to Apollos and Paul. In verse 3 the reference becomes wholly personal. The term "judged" technically denotes an examination rather than a judgment, but this examination results in a sentence, and the word "judge" is an effective translation. "Human court" is literally "a human day." Here "day" is used in the sense of the day of judgment, and, by analogy with the Day of the Lord, the term refers to the judgment itself. Paul has stated that he has no interest in the judgment of the Corinthians or any other human being about him. It does not matter to him whether or not these judgments exist. This is not a disparaging remark about the abilities of the Corinthians to conduct judgments, but it demonstrates the incompetency of all human beings to judge. As a further example of Paul's indifference toward human assessment of his accomplishments, he states that he does not pass judgment on himself. Paul is not prohibiting self-evaluation but is warning against a decisive, final judgment that will justify or condemn a person on account of his works. He is concerned that such a judgment would usurp God's place of judgment, for within him "there are unexplored recesses which do not allow him to discover thoroughly the real state of things, the full integrity of his own fidelity, and consequently to pronounce a valid sentence on himself" (Godet). Bruce expresses his insights in the following words:

> A trustworthy steward need not trouble greatly about the opinions of others, provided his master is satisfied with him. Members of the Corinthian church might put Paul high or low down on their list of favourite ministers; but this was a matter of little consequence in his eyes . . . ; even his own self-assessment was ultimately immaterial, although in this as in other respects he endeavoured to preserve a good conscience.

In verse 4 Paul indicates that he does not know of a failure in his service, but he relies on God's judgment to provide a proper verdict. In the fact of his ignorance before God Paul can put no confidence. He means that he has at present no guilty secret to share with himself. This fact, however, speaks more of his ignorance than of his innocence. An unaccusing conscience does not mean the absence of guilt. Only God has adequate insight to evaluate the true sources of action and service. Paul's words should not be viewed as a vain boast, for the apostle did not intend to proclaim his spiritual sinlessness. He stated that his conscience did not prick him with a pressing awareness of unfaithfulness. Doubtless God could have flashed before Paul innumerable instances of disobedience in his own life.

The conclusion to these warnings is introduced by the "therefore" of verse 5. The Corinthians are to stop judging. The fact that they were already judging is evident from the use in Greek of a present imperative to express this prohibition. Any present judgment will be partial, premature, and incompetent. Only the judgment of the Lord can uncover the true acts and motives of the individual. In Paul's letter there is frequent reference to the prospect of having his apostolic service reviewed by the Lord at the parousia (2 Cor. 1:14; 5:9,10; Phil. 2:16), and an awareness of these facts was doubtless a significant incentive toward godly effort. Godet suggests that "what is hidden in darkness" refer to the full revelation of the acts of an individual. The "motives of men's hearts" are seen as a reference to the motives prompting these acts. When these factors are examined, the result will be praise from God. Bruce notes that the word used by Paul for "praise" is a positive word rather than a more neutral word that could refer to good or bad awards. "The implication may be that the Lord in his omniscience will find cause for approval where another judge would find none."

It is interesting to distinguish three separate judgments mentioned in this section. Verse 3 speaks of a judgment passed on us by others. In verse 4 there is a reference to the judgment of one's own conscience. In verses 4 and 5 we find a discussion of the Lord's judgment. Only the Lord's judgment carries any concern for Paul. Since God can see the totality of actions and the springs of the will prompting them, He can judge with exacting precision and bypass all of man's pompous pretenses to reward. He can also find grounds for reward when skeptical human beings would find none.

3. Human pride (4:6–13)

Paul concludes his explanation of the reasons for the factions by suggesting in verses 6 and 7 that the leaders of the factions should be able to see their own pride in the illustrations he has been using of himself and Apollos. Further, he uses irony in verses 8–13 to point out that the apostles about whom they had been debating were little more than "fools for Christ."

In the foregoing passages Paul has used various metaphors—agricultural workers, builders, servants, and stewards. He has applied all of these to himself and to Apollos so that the Corinthians might learn to practice humility and to banish pride. Paul's mention of Apollos (v. 6) suggests that there were friendly relations between them, and Paul is also careful not to mention anything that might be seen as criticism of Peter. The word for "applied" means to present a thing or a person in a form different from its natural figure so as to alter or disguise it. Paul means that in the passages from 3:5 on he has been presenting truths and relating them outwardly to Apollos and himself while intending them for certain teachers and for a church.

The phrase, "beyond what is written," in verse 6 is a formula that Paul frequently uses in quoting Scripture. There is no Old Testament passage with exactly the idea of 4:6, but Morris feels that "Paul will be referring to the general sense of the Old Testament." He is directing their attention to the fact that they must learn the scriptural idea of the subordination of man and cease to think too highly of him. All his efforts had attempted to prevent their practice of partisanship. "He desires that they have no feelings of pride as they contemplate the particular teacher to whom they have attached themselves" (Morris). His use of the present tense in "take pride in" suggests that a condition that ought not to be was in progress then in Corinth. Paul moves in verse 7 to show what is to be condemned in becoming proud.

The "for" of verse 7 introduces a reason why conceit is out of place. Paul handles his objections by asking three questions: Who makes one of you superior to another? What do you have that has not been given to you? Why boast in what you have been given? Here Paul's thought has moved into the area of gifts received from God, and he is not dealing with instructions received from teachers. The teachers about whom the Corinthians were glorying were but ministers of the grace of God. The proper attitude to be shown was humble gratitude. Knox renders the first question with the words: "After all, friend, who is it that gives thee this preeminence?" Phillips catches the spirit of the third question with: "Why boast of it as if it were something you had achieved yourself?" In the next verses the sin of the Corinthians becomes so vivid for Paul that his conversation with them moves into a long expression of polite sarcasm.

His words in verse 8 use irony to attack the self-esteem of his readers. Robertson and Plummer see the first three verbs of verse 8 as forming a climax in which the highly blessed Corinthians are seen as already in the kingdom of God and enjoying its banquets and treasures. The phrase "all you want" is used frequently of food and denotes satiation, a feeling of satisfaction. In contrast with Jesus' appeal to hunger and thirst after righteousness in Matthew 5:6 the Corinthians felt no lack. The next two verbs show the fancied security and absence of a sense of need in the Corinthians. Jesus' words to the Laodicean church (Rev. 3:17) show how dangerous this is.

Paul's teaching had suggested that suffering would precede glory (Rom. 8:16–17). Bruce feels that some of the Corinthians resorted to an "over-realized" eschatology, and that they felt they had already attained the kingdom and glory of Christ at the same time that they received the Spirit of God. They would thus have bypassed suffering and achieved glory. Paul's sarcastic response in verse 8 indicates that it is a pity that they are wrong because he and his fellow apostles would like to believe that suffering was a thing of the past.

Instead of reigning, the apostles actually suffered many trials and were humiliated in it all. For Paul the suffering of the apostles is still a present experience (v. 9). He was not complaining about this fact, for he was eager to experience personally the afflictions of Christ to relieve his fellow Christians (2 Cor. 1:4–7; 4:11,12; Col. 1:24). He compared the lot of the apostles to that of men who were sentenced to death, like condemned criminals in the amphitheater. The word "spectacle" was normally the place where plays or spectacles were presented. Paul is saying that the apostles were being exhibited as a spectacle to a world that consisted of angels and men. Robertson and Plummer suggest that Paul is thinking of "a great pageant in which the Apostles form the ignominious finale, consisting of doomed men, who will have to fight in the arena till they are killed." It is a disgraceful picture for the apostle to consider for himself.

The implications of being made such a spectacle are brought out in verse 10. Paul uses three pairs of contrasting adjectives that fall on the proud Corinthians like so many blows. The words would be spoken to the principal men of Corinth, but they would also prick the members of the church who share the pretensions of their leaders. The first pair of adjectives forms an antithesis with reference to teaching. The apostles had to encounter the reputation for foolishness, and the Corinthians, by contrast, tried to find a way to preach Christ so as to obtain a reputation for wisdom and pretentious loftiness. If Paul had remained true to his work as a rabbi, he might have become as celebrated as a Gamaliel or a Hillel. Instead, he consented to pass as a fool. The Corinthians managed to make their teaching of the gospel a means of gaining personal esteem.

The second pair of adjectives related to general conduct. The demeanor of the apostles was weak as witnessed in Paul's description in 2:1–5. The Corinthians appear in public with the feeling of their strength. There is no hesitation or timidity in them.

The third pair of antithetical adjectives related to their worldly position. The Corinthians are honored and are seen as the ornament of cultivated circles. The apostles are despised, reviled, and excoriated. The word "dishonored" now becomes a theme that Paul paints with reference to the apostles in verses 11–13.

Williams translates verse 11 as: "To this very hour we have gone hungry, thirsty, poorly clad; we have been roughly knocked around, we have had no home." For Paul these disgraces were going on up to that very moment. There was no relief from labor and suffering in his life. Verse 11 suggests that Paul and the apostles lacked suitable food, water, and clothing. To be "brutally treated" was to be struck with the fist just as Christ was (Matt. 26:67). The word showing that Paul was "homeless" does not appear elsewhere in the New Testament. Robertson and Plummer suggest that it means that "they were vagrants, and were stigmatized as such." Paul is relating all of these difficulties to remind the Corinthians just how far removed he and the apostles are from reigning. He is warning the Corinthians against their pride and is summoning them to imitate him.

The hard work of verse 12 refers to labor to the point of exhaustion. The MLB suggests that it means: "We toil to exhaustion with our own hands." Barrett points out that the word for "work hard" is used by Paul for specifically Christian work such as the labor of preaching and caring for the churches (Col. 1:29). The word may thus refer to his practice of supporting himself by his craft without making an appeal for help from his converts. Paul would thus be saying that he did his Christian work and also supported himself by secular work. The Greeks who despised manual labor would detest such behavior in a teacher, but Paul glories in it. The word "cursed" is used in 1 Peter 2:23 to describe the sufferings of Christ. When Paul and the apostles were treated as Jesus had been treated, they obeyed His injunction in Luke 6:28 to bless their accusers. Phillips renders the last pair of verbs in verse 12 as: "They make our lives miserable, but we take it patiently."

Williams suggests that the opening verbs of verse 13 should be translated: "When we are slandered by them we try to conciliate them." The Greeks would see this as cowardliness, but Paul sees this as a demonstration of the virtues of Christianity. The word "scum" can be used of the impurities that are removed and thrown away whenever a vessel is cleansed. The word was occasionally used of a worthless human being on whom the guilt of a community was unloaded. Bruce mentions that this use of the word "would fit in well with his comparison of the apostles to the condemned criminals in the amphitheatre." The word "refuse" may also be used of vile criminals whose blood was shed by pagans to avert the wrath of the gods.

Paul's strong words were inspired by an indignation that saw the state of spiritual life in Corinth as a mortal danger to the life and future of the church. Further, the weapon of ridicule or irony was often quite effective against the problem of proud infatuation that Paul found in the city. Perhaps these penetrating words could be softened somewhat by the tenderness and compassion displayed in verses 14–21. Here Paul brought to a conclusion all he has written from 1:12 on.

D. Appeal for Reconciliation (4:14–21)

Paul's words in these verses are based on his special relationship with the Corinthians. They are his beloved children, and in Christ Jesus he has begotten them through the gospel. He wants them to understand that the severe words he has just spoken are not inspired by resentment or hatred but reflect his deep concern for them.

Williams renders the thought of verse 14 as: "I do not write this to make you blush with shame but to give you counsel as my dear children." The word "shame" means literally to "turn one's back upon himself," and, by deduction from this, "to cause shame." Perhaps Paul had seemed to speak to them in a humiliating way, but he truly wanted to lead them firmly in another direction. Later, in 6:5, he does speak with the view of making them ashamed. Here he desires to admonish them. He wants to bring their mind back to a calm and settled place. He is the only one of the teachers who is their spiritual father and who can address them as "my dear children." The next verse tries to justify his position as father.

The "guardian" or "tutor" of verse 15 was the Roman pedagogue who took the child of patrician families to school and looked after him. He might dearly love the child, but he was not the father and thus lacked fatherly affection for him. The teachers whom Paul had mentioned in these verses were related to the Corinthians as a pedagogue to the child, but only Paul was their father. Paul's missionary work had led them to become Christians. He had not begotten them in his own right, for Christ was the agent of their conversion, and the gospel was the means by which they had been brought to new life. Not only does Paul have the right to admonish them, but as their father he has a duty.

In verse 16 Paul urges the Corinthians to become his imitators. He is not recruiting personal followers in the sense of 1:12, but he wants them to imitate him so that they might imitate Christ (11:1; 1 Thess. 1:6). The life of the apostle had been a clear reflection of Christ crucified, and on other occasions he appealed to his readers to imitate him as a means of duplicating the behavior of the Lord (Phil. 3:17; 2 Thess. 3:7,9). Robertson and Plummer note that "the charge is not given in a spirit of self-confidence. He has received the charge to lead them, and he is bound to set an example for them to follow." Individual believers should show such an obedience to Christ that they should not fear to say modestly, "Follow me even as I follow the Lord."

Timothy had probably set out on the journey mentioned by Paul in verse 17, for the absence of his name from the salutation in 1:1 would suggest this. There is a later reference to Timothy's visit in 16:10 and 11, and this trip may also be referred to in Acts 19:22. Timothy was a product of Paul's first missionary journey (Acts 16:1–5) and had become one of

Paul's closest associates. Paul's appreciation of his character and service is mentioned in Philippians 2:20–22, but the admonitions of 2 Timothy 1:6–9 suggest some of Timothy's shortcomings. Timothy was being sent to remind his hearers of the truths and ethical principles that Paul had also demanded elsewhere. In other passages of 1 Corinthians Paul showed his concern that all his churches should exhibit the same standards of Christian practice (7:17; 11:16; 14:33). Paul had a general consistency in his teaching, and Timothy could lead the Corinthians to understand this. The sending of Timothy might cause some to suppose that Timothy was a substitute for Paul. They might conclude that Paul would not consider coming himself. Paul notes that some of the Corinthians were exulting in this possibility, and he deals with this insulting suggestion in verses 18–21.

The words "become arrogant" in verse 18 refer "to the air of triumph" with which Paul's opponents in Corinth greeted the idea that Paul was not coming (Godet). Godet sees these opponents as members of the "Christ" party, for Paul's references to opposition in 2 Corinthians seem to picture them in that way (2 Cor. 10:7; 11:23). In 2 Corinthians there is also evidence that Paul's opponents charged him with frightening the church by writing threatening letters (2 Cor. 10:9–10) with the implication that in person he would be unimpressive and cowardly. Paul had exercised restraint with the Corinthians, and some of the church members may have practiced license in his absence. They had overlooked the possibility of his return, and they saw themselves as masters of the situation. Paul's next words would be jarring to such people.

In verse 19 Paul promises to come to Corinth shortly, and only divine restraint will prevent his appearance. When he comes, he will examine the pompous words of the Corinthians. The phrase "find out" is the language of a judge who sets about to make an examination. Here the expression "talking" refers to the lofty discourses, eloquent tirades, and profound speeches that some of the Corinthians had used. Paul is not interested in these, but he is concerned about the actual power in their lives. He wants to know if they have the humility and compassion of the Holy Spirit. Detecting this is a field in which Paul is an expert, and they will not be able to deceive him at this point. Some of those who were "arrogant" will later be rebuked by Paul in the words of 5:2. Taylor renders the latter half of verse 19 as: "I'll find out whether these proud men are just big talkers or whether they really have God's power."

The kingdom of God is not a reference to the messianic kingdom but to the spiritual kingdom of God that already lives in the souls of believers (v. 20). God's reign spiritually in the heart of the humble believer will prepare the way for its future appearance. The rule of God in the heart of the individual is not a matter of high-powered words and fine advice. There must be power in the individual to live a godly life with full dependence on the strength that God can provide (Gal. 5:22–24). Conybeare translates the verse as: "For mighty deeds, not empty words, are the tokens of God's kingdom."

The question was not whether Paul would come, but how he would come (v. 21). That would be settled by the response of the Corinthians. Paul's use of "whip" suggests that he sensed the need for disciplinary action among the Corinthians. He might rebuke or chastise them. The combination of "love and with a gentle spirit" suggests that Paul will come in this manner if the Corinthians humble themselves and repent of their prideful ways. Even if Paul came with the whip, he would still come in love. The question is whether the love is to be expressed in gentleness or violence. Not the mood of Paul, but the response of the Corinthians will determine this.

The references to the coming visit of Timothy and his own visit would be suitable for ending the letter. Paul may have been preparing to conclude this letter when further news arrived from Corinth about problems that needed addressing. The news may have been brought by the bearers of the letter that he answers in 7:1, and these bearers may have been Stephanas, Fortunatas, and Achaicus (16:17).

For Further Study

1. Read articles on "Wisdom," "Mystery," "Holy Spirit," "Minister," and "Steward" in *The Zondervan Pictorial Encyclopedia of the Bible.*

2. Read 1 Corinthians 1:18–24 and then put in parallel columns the terms that Paul, Jews, and Greeks would use to refer to the gospel. Can you define these terms?

3. Read 1 Corinthians 2:14–3:4 and then define Paul's use of the terms "natural," "spiritual," and "carnal" as applied to different types of Christians.

4. After a careful reading of 3:5–4:5 list some of the false conceptions of the Christian ministry that Paul was exposing in this section.

5. Using Paul's words in 4:9–13, list some of the difficulties of the ministry that Paul shared with the Corinthians.

Chapter 3

Moral Problems
(1 Corinthians 5:1–6:20)

The church at Corinth was filled with problems stemming from immaturity, lack of brotherly love, and moral shamelessness. This section begins the apostle's treatment of some of these problems.

The shocking absence of moral discipline in the church is seen by its condoning an instance of incest (5:1–13). The Corinthian problem of being "arrogant" lay beneath this disorder. This sin of pride also produced the party spirit to which Paul has devoted much of his previous discussion. Paul had learned of the problem and had decided, even though absent from the church, on the method for dealing with it and shared his directive to the church. He also attempted (vv. 9–13) to correct a misunderstanding that some earlier instructions may have caused.

The lack of brotherly love is seen by the practice of Christians going to law with each other before unbelievers (6:1–11). It was bad enough to have disagreements, but this was compounded by taking them to a pagan judge for solution. Paul suggests that the Corinthians take a loss rather than go to court (6:7–8), and he urges them to abandon all their past unrighteousness (6:9–11).

The moral shamelessness of Corinth is further seen by the church's toleration of sexual immorality (6:12–20). Paul reminds his readers that their bodies belong to the Lord and are truly the temples of the Holy Spirit. Since God has purchased the Corinthians at a high cost, they are to glorify Him in their bodies.

A. Incest (5:1–13)

Here Paul presents the facts of the case that had been brought to his attention (vv. 1,2). The presence of the problem was a spiritual humiliation, but their prideful response was even more an embarrassment. In verses 3–8 Paul directed that the unrepentant offender be removed from the fellowship lest his behavior defile and pollute others. Paul further explained his words in verses 9–13 so that his readers would know that his command to separate from immoral people was seen to refer to professing believers and not to immoral pagans.

1. *Facts of the case* (5:1–2)

The words "sexual immorality" in verse 1 are a reference to sexual irregularity of almost any kind. The word "actually" expresses shock at the nature of the rumor. The type of immorality mentioned would not have been sanctioned even by pagans. The accusation probably does not pertain to a son who seduced his mother. If this had been true, Paul would likely have said so. "Whether it means that the offender had seduced his step-mother, or that she was divorced from his father, or that the father had died, leaving her a widow, is not clear" (Morris). What is apparent is that an illicit liaison of a scandalous nature had taken place. The present tense used with "has" suggests that the case of sexual irregularity was not an isolated incident but was perhaps a permanent union of some kind. It was not a formal marriage, but it resembled "common-law" marriages of today. The woman was likely not a believer, for only the male offender is rebuked. Paul would regard the behavior of the Christian as the concern of the church and would thus speak to it. Godet quotes Cicero in a Roman opinion of the unsavory nature of incest: "O incredible crime for a woman, and such as has never been heard of in this world in any other than her solitary case." Cicero is not referring to the incident here, but his words of pain show the horror of enlightened pagans at such practice.

The conceited self-satisfaction of the Corinthians led them to condone this practice of incest. Their being "proud" may refer to a spiritual confusion that led them to view themselves as spiritual persons so that what they did with their bodies no longer mattered. Bruce feels that a significant number in the church felt "that this was rather a fine assertion of Christian liberty, of emancipation from Jewish law and Gentile convention alike." Paul insists that the circumstances do not call for arrogance but for weeping. Phillips translates the last section of verse 2 as: "The man who has done such a thing should certainly be expelled from your fellowship." Godet, however, sees the reference as describing a mourning by the church so that God might act to remove the guilty party from their midst as seen in a case such as that of Ananias and Sapphira (Acts 5:1–11). Sickness or death might result from such a divine visitation by God. Paul had spoken of the people of Corinth as "sanctified in Christ Jesus and called to be holy." How could one guilty of incest have a place in such an assembly?

2. Action to be taken (5:3–8)

The Corinthians, who were near to the problem, might have been expected to take the initiative. They had done nothing, and Paul, at a distance, had decided to take strong measures (v. 3). Paul was not in Corinth physically, but he was psychologically. The Corinthians would easily remember some of Paul's directives, actions, and warnings about such evil when he ministered among them, and that would add to Paul's spiritual presence. Paul views himself as president of an assembly and has already passed sentence. The verb for "passed judgment" is a perfect tense, and this gives an air of finality to the sentence. Paul does not name the guilty person, but he characterizes him by the nature of his actions.

Paul's words in verse 4 suggest a solemn assembly called for the purpose of administering disciplinary action. Godet does not see this as a church business meeting that might issue a decree of excommunication after debating and a majority vote. He sees this as a solemn execration, the binding referred to by Jesus in Matthew 18:18–20. "It is a spiritual act in which, from the very nature of things, only the man takes part who feels impelled to it, and each in the measure in which he is capable of it" (Godet). The Corinthians and the spirit of Paul are to meet together in the name of the Lord Jesus Christ. Paul's spiritual presence would be present, as discussed in verse 3. This assembly is to meet in the name of the Lord Jesus, under His authority, and with the intention of obeying Him. They are to carry out their work with the power of the Lord Jesus. It is this power that carries the decision of the assembly into execution. The act thus accomplished will be the act of the church and not merely of Paul. Paul's effort here is to lead the church to assume its responsibility for its people.

The action of this assembly is mentioned in verse 5 as delivering the offender to Satan. The purpose of this deliverance is the salvation of the man (v. 5) and the removal of evil from the church (vv. 6–8). This action has two common interpretations. It may refer to excommunication, expelling the guilty person from the community in which Christ is Lord into that realm that is dominated by the god of this age (2 Cor. 4:4; 1 Tim. 1:20). Or it may refer to the inflicting of physical illness or even death on the man. Here again there are parallels in the instance of Ananias and Sapphira (Acts 5:1–11) and that of Elymas the sorcerer (Acts 13:8–12). Bruce notes that the "language implies a severer sentence than excommunication" and supports his point in his interpretation of "the destruction of the flesh." Some would see the "flesh" as a reference to the lower nature of the sinner. The idea is that putting the offender in the realm of

Satan might destroy the flesh as the source of personal evil by letting the offender experience the contrast between living among the people of God and living under the rule of the flesh. Presumably, he would soon learn that he wanted to be free of a bad taskmaster. Bruce sees the destruction of the flesh as referring to the physical consequences of the act of excommunication and suggests that it might mean more than mere affliction or sickness. He notes that it might mean death here and now. Paul does mention in 11:30 sickness and death as the result of another kind of sin. The decision and ban of the congregation might have been self-fulfilling as the prophetic word of the Old Testament. Some see that the offender here is referred to in 2 Corinthians 2:5–11, but the length of time between the writing of the two letters is such that the identification is unlikely.

The purpose for this action is that the spirit may be "saved on the day of the Lord." Paul obviously means this in the sense of full salvation, for the act of salvation is to be made known in the day of the Lord Jesus. It was Paul's hope that the punishment inflicted by this church on an erring member might result eventually in his salvation. The ultimate goal of Paul in mentioning this punishment is thus remedial and not merely punitive. Paul also is concerned that the evil example of this offender be removed as a source of temptation for the church, and he now moves to discuss this idea (vv. 6–8).

The words of Paul provide much grist for the modern church to ponder. Discipline such as Paul describes here is almost unknown in the church of today. Findley Edge has suggested four reasons for this (pp. 223–25). He notes that sin is so prevalent in the lives of the members that the church does not know where to start. Also, he admits that the practice of church discipline would be a major disruptive force in the life of the church. Further, he observes that there has been a revolt against the flagrant abuses of past practices of church discipline. Finally, he states that Christians today have a low view of what it means to be the church. He suggests that the church should not view discipline merely as punitive but also as formative and redemptive. If the church were to use discipline to form patterns of purity in the lives of its members, it would be less necessary to consider its use in the punitive or reformative sense. He suggests that the church should institute a waiting period before granting membership and indicts Christians for their lack of love, for "by failing to practice discipline, the church is admitting that it does not love its own enough to go through the painful process of seeking their reclamation" (Edge, p. 238).

In verses 6–8 Paul uses the imagery of the Passover to emphasize the urgency for removing evil from the congregation. In the circumstances of immorality overt boasting would seem out of place, but the Corinthians were guilty of it. They had likely minimized the entire incident, and Paul asserts its threat to the very life of the church. Leaven is used in the Scripture as a symbol of evil. Paul asserts that a small quantity of leaven would be enough to impregnate an entire lump of dough. Similarly one corrupt member could corrupt an entire church. In verse 7 the quotation of the saying about leaven reminds Paul of the Jewish custom of clearing out the old leaven from the house prior to the Passover. In this a completely new start is made with the next year's grain (Exod. 12:15; 13:6–7), and the first batch of dough from which new bread was made is therefore a new lump, completely unleavened. After the Feast of Unleavened Bread, new leaven would be introduced into the house. By virtue of their turning to Christ these Christians were now a new creation, a new lump (2 Cor. 5:17), and they should live this out in their own experience. Paul calls the Corinthians "without yeast," and he means that by virtue of their calling as God's holy people, they were to be holy in life. Here the imperative calling for holiness is unthinkable without the indicative stating that they are holy.

In the Passover celebration the search for leaven was undertaken before the slaying of the victim. In the instance of the Corinthians Christ had already been sacrificed, and it was high time they remove the leaven. The moral actions of the Corinthians were to catch up with the initiative that God had taken.

In verse 8 Paul pictures the Christian life with the symbols of a festival. In participating in this festival the Corinthians are to remove the leaven of malice and evil, the standards of the old life. They are to show the sincerity that comes from pure motives and the godly action that results from practicing the truth. The sin from which they had been rescued must be a thing of the past, and holiness must become the abiding quality of the present and future. Paul may well have written 1 Corinthians near the time of Passover (10:1; 15:20; 16:8), and this would add strength to his use of paschal metaphors.

3. *Explanation* (5:9–13)

Paul's stern words about immorality now lead him to make a clarification concerning some previously given instructions. Most commentators feel that the "letter" mentioned in verse 9 is a letter to the Corinthians antedating 1 Corinthians and now lost. In 1 Corinthians Paul has not given any instructions about not associating with fornicators. His instructions to the church concerning a man who has practiced incest could not be seen as prohibiting contact with fornicators. Bruce points out that the misunderstanding of the Corinthians may have been deliberate (p. 57). They may have raised the objection of the impossibility of being separate from evil as an effort to excuse them from making a serious effort to deal with evil.

In verse 10 Paul explains that in this world it is impossible to avoid mixing with some evil men. The "greedy" were those who desired to have more. The "swindlers" were those who seized something belonging to others, robbers. These would have had a wrong relation to God. Williams translates the verse: "Not that you are to stop all dealings with sexually immoral people of this world, any more than with its greedy graspers, or its idolators, for then you would have to get clear out of the world." Bruce reminds us that "a Corinthian Christian could not choose his butcher, his baker, or even his next-door neighbour, on the basis of his morals." Such a lack of contact between Christians and unsaved outsiders would assure that many of these would never learn about the Lord of life. Surely Paul did not desire that!

In verses 11–13 Paul makes it clear that he is talking of the professing Christian who practices immorality. Paul urges his readers not to keep company with one who professes to be a Christian but who denies his profession by his manner of life. In verse 11 Paul introduces two new nouns to describe classes of immoral people. A "slanderer" was a person who abused others. A "drunkard" was someone given over to drink. Paul commands the Corinthians that they must not even maintain social fellowship with such compromising Christians, and the prohibition would certainly apply to fellowship in the observance of the Lord's Supper. Hopefully Paul's commands would prevent the spread of evil and bring offenders to see the error of their ways. Paul's words should not be seen as prohibiting social contact today with a view to rescuing wavering Christians, but it warns against association with flagrantly immoral people who profess to be Christians.

Paul states the principle in verse 12 that the Christian has no right to pass censorious judgment on those outside the fellowship. The church does have the responsibility for its own members. There was to be strict discipline within the church but freedom of association outside of it. The judgment that Paul discusses is related to the discipline of the membership and is not a substitute for God's penetrating final judgment. The plural "you" reminds the Corinthians that the responsibility for this judgment belongs to the entire church. What Paul urges is not censoriousness but the discipline of the church membership. He explains the role of God as being responsible for the judgment of those outside the church, presumably at the last day. He is the judge of all the earth (Gen. 18:25). The command to exclude "the wicked man" is a reference to the exclusion of the offender, not to Satan. Origen aptly adds that we must not be content with expelling the evil man from our society, but we must also expel the evil one from our hearts (Robertson and Plummer, p. 108).

B. Dealings With Heathen Courts (6:1–11)

The subject of discipline was connected with the realm of congregational life, but it touches on moral questions, with which Paul now comes to deal more specifically. In 5:1–13 he had asserted that the church had a mission to judge those within its membership, but he indicated that God judged those outside. He now scores the church for submitting personal differences for judgment to those who are spiritually beneath them, outsiders, the unregenerate. What a travesty for Christians to submit personal grievances before those who lack the light of the gospel!

1. A rebuke (6:1–8)

Paul's word "dare" in verse 1 expresses shock. Was there someone among the Corinthians who exhibited this miserable courage? The phrase, "has a dispute with" is a technical expression for a lawsuit. Paul recognizes that such disputes will occur, but he wants them to be settled within the brotherhood. The Jews, puffed up by their own theocratic nobility, did not resort to appearances before heathen judges. They established a system of arbitration among themselves for deciding such questions. The Corinthians lacked enough Christian honor to rise to the same level. The term "ungodly" is used to refer to those who did not regulate their thinking and living by God's laws. They were not righteous in the sight of God. Paul does not imply that Christians would not receive justice from these judges but that they had no business appearing before the heathen justice bar at all. He was not suggesting that a Christian boycott an appearance before lawfully constituted authority. He himself had appeared with much success before Gallio (Acts 18:12–17), but he did not want Christians to bring their differences to a pagan judge for settlement. The saints should settle such matters among themselves.

The expectation that the "saints will judge the world" may be derived from Daniel 7:22, where judgment is given to the saints of the "Most High." The reference is to a final judicial act in the last days. Paul's prohibition in 5:12 against judging outsiders refers to earthly and temporal judgments, but here he is stating that Christians will be involved in God's final judgment of the unbelievers. If Christians are to be involved in such momentous final judgments, why should they act as if unworthy to settle such trivial matters as earthly differences? Paul does not suggest clearly the areas over which the Corinthians were quibbling, but he likely refers to money, property, and such business matters. Robertson and Plummer question whether Paul is using "judge" in the sense of "pronounce a judgment upon." They feel that the word might be used with its Hebraic idea of "ruling." Even if this interpretation is accepted, it will not affect the argument of Paul who is contending for the competency of Christians to handle matters relating to this life.

In verse 3 Paul raises the previous argument of verse 2 to its highest point. Beings of such an exalted nature as angels will one day be subjected to the jurisdiction of believers. This statement by Paul cannot be paralleled elsewhere in Scripture and, like the truths mentioned in 1 Thessalonians 4:13–18, rests on a personal revelation to him. Paul is reminding the Christians that they were going to court about mere trifles compared to the responsibility involved in judging angels. If they can judge the highest class of created beings, they have the competence to handle everyday affairs relating to money and business disagreements.

Paul uses irony to drive home a point in verse 4. His statements may be seen as either a question or a command. If this is a question, Paul asks the Corinthians why they approach those least regarded by the church? In this instance he would be referring to pagan judges who have no status in the church, but it seems strange to refer to them as least esteemed when such judges would have no esteem at all. The clause may be seen as a command by Paul to take the least esteemed church members and allow them to judge the trivial disputes that are arising within the fellowship. This sounds like rather ridiculous irony, but in verse 5 Paul indicates that he is attempting to shame the Christians into changing their actions. His irony may have been intentional. The members "of little account" may lack the competence to handle the more serious duties of church government, but Paul sees them as competent to handle the disputes that he now discusses.

In verse 5 Paul's use of the word "judge" pictures a case of arbitration in which a brother seeks to settle different claims among Christians. Paul is suggesting that Christian arbitration be used rather than heathen tribunals. The sad conclusion of the affair is outlined in verse 6. It was a scandal before the heathen world that Christians should go to law with Christians before unbelievers. The use of unbelievers meant that no one from among their own company was wise enough to arbitrate between one Christian and another. It was sad enough to have disagreements appearing among Christians. It was even more scandalous that Christians should seek to settle them with the help of unbelievers. The tense of the verb "judge" in verse 5 is an aorist. It reflects the verdict given by an arbitrator, a verdict that is past. The tense in verse 6 of "goes to law" is a present tense. It reflects the lengthy, labyrinthine developments of a tangled lawsuit. That was an act between brothers and before a heathen tribunal! It was continuously going on. Shame to the church!

In verses 7 and 8 Paul suggests an alternate means of settling the process. Going to law with a fellow Christian was actually a defeat. Paul is not suggesting that a Christian take no steps to insulate himself against injustice. However, if it must come to a lawsuit, the Christian ought to be prepared to bear the wrong. Paul may be referring to Jesus' words in Matthew 5:39–42. The two verbs for "be wronged" and "be cheated" are in the middle voice and suggest that the Christians should let themselves be wronged and defrauded. They must take steps to see that this is done. To "be wronged" is used to refer to general injustices, and to "be cheated" is used of wrongs in regard to property. Even by appearing in court an argument for the Christian position had been overthrown and had been replaced by selfish desire. In verse 8 Paul clearly points out that the Corinthian Christians had double problems. They sinned against ethical standards, for they actually defrauded. They also wounded brotherly love. Williams states the truth as: "You practice wronging and robbing others, and that your brothers." The Corinthians who had received much grace now behaved as if they had no moral responsibility. Paul points out this dangerous misunderstanding (vv. 9–11).

2. A warning (6:9–11)

The Corinthians acted as if their pious chatter would open heaven to them regardless of their conduct. Their falling back into sin showed that they may have been deceived about their profession of regeneration. Those who claimed to have been washed may have returned to wallow in the mud (2 Peter 2:22). The identity of the "wicked" is defined by the list that follows. In content, this list resembles the "acts of the sinful nature" listed in Galatians 5:19–21. There the warning is given that those who do such things will not inherit the kingdom of God. The "kingdom of God" is a reference to the eschatological dimension of the term. It speaks of the final consummation of God's plan for the ages and not merely of the present state that moves toward that goal. Paul's prohibition against being deceived suggests that the specious arguments then current in Corinth had indeed misled some of the Corinthians. "Do not be deceived!" is the warning of Paul. The first five terms in Paul's list relate to impurity, often to sexual impurity (v. 9). The words for "sexually immoral" and "idolators" have appeared in 5:10–11, and "sexual immorality" has appeared in 5:1. The "adulterers" are those who violate the marriage bed. The "male prostitutes" and the "homosexual offenders" are taken by Barrett as catamites and sodomites, the passive and active partners respectively in homosexual relations. The next five terms relate to those who spoil the goods of others (v. 10). The "thieves" are seen by Morris as "petty pilferers, sneak-thieves, rather than brigands." The remaining words have already appeared in 5:10 and 11. Godet reminds us that "the kingdom of God is a holy state of things, it receives none but sanctified members."

In verse 11 Paul indicates that some of the Corinthians had indeed been guilty of these practices in their pre-Christian days. The verb for "washed" could be a reference to the act of baptism or to a washing in the blood of Christ (Rev. 1:5). If the reference is to baptism, the act would be pictured as a symbol of the spiritual graces involved in being sanctified and justified. The middle voice of the verb for "washed" emphasizes the "freedom and spontaneity with which they had done the deed" (Godet). The tenses of the verbs for "sanctified" and "justified" are aorists. This would refer to a deed performed once for all and not to something continually underway. Sanctification is that initial act by which the believer is taken from a state of corruption to a state of holiness. Justification is the bestowal of righteousness made available through faith in Christ. The tense of the verb for "justified" makes it difficult to see the word as referring to the practical righteousness of daily living. It should rather be seen as describing that righteousness imputed to the Christian at his moment of conversion. The reference to "the name of the Lord Jesus Christ" shows that the work of grace in the Corinthians depends on what God had done in Jesus. The "Spirit of our God" is mentioned to identify the agent of sanctification. Paul was appealing to the Corinthians to become as holy and righteous in their daily practice as they already were theologically by their experience of faith in Jesus Christ.

C. Abuse of Christian Freedom (6:12–20)

In verse 9 Paul had warned the Corinthians against being deceived, and then he began to deal with the subject of impurity, specifically sexual impurity. The emphasis on deception allows him to enter the subject with renewed vigor in this section. Some Corinthians were twisting strangely the meaning of salvation by grace and were condoning the practice of evil by an appeal to Christian liberty. Paul will tolerate none of this nonsense, and he proceeds to explain why.

Paul's phrase, "Everything is permissible for me," is tossed out as if it were a familiar slogan of the Christians. He is probably quoting the Corinthians who used this statement to justify their immorality. Barrett feels that they "were the watchword of a gnostic party in Corinth." If this were the source, the views would not reflect a more fully developed gnosticism of the second century but an incipient form. Gnosticism disparaged the material body, and this position may have led some to feel that they could do anything they wished to the body. Another view of the source of the words is that the Corinthians were quoting words Paul had used. Against Jewish legalism Paul may have contended for liberty with words like these, and his opponents may have taken his doctrine of liberty to an extreme. Paul corrects this misunderstanding by showing that "everything" is not to be taken without some qualification.

Paul's response wages battle on two fronts (Bruce). With the libertines Paul agrees that all is lawful, but he adds that not everything is useful or expedient in the Christian life. With the ascetics he also agrees that all things are lawful, but he warns that these things can acquire authority over and dominate an individual. Paul's words apply only in the area where there is no explicit moral command in Scripture. He would never have referred them to the Ten Commandments. Outside of things expressly forbidden in Scripture the believer is not surrounded with a multitude of restrictions. However, some of these things are not helpful and some can enslave. Paul develops the implications of this second restriction in verses 13–17.

The words of verse 13 through "God will destroy them both" may contain another slogan. Perhaps Paul found it in Corinth and dealt with it as pertinent to his argument. The words suggest that food goes into the stomach where it is decomposed into its elements. Eventually the body will be dissolved at death. Eating food, therefore, has no eternal significance. Some must have argued that just as the transiency of the body and foods allowed a Christian to eat without regard to food laws, he could also satisfy his sexual appetite most conveniently (Barrett). Paul agrees that the belly and eating go together, but not the body and fornication. The belly has no permanence, but the body for Paul is man as a whole, and this body has permanency. The body is human personality, and it is to be used for the Lord (Rom. 12:1). The Lord and the body are to be permanently united, both in the weakness of this age (2 Cor. 12:9–10) and in the glory of the life beyond (2 Cor. 5:1–5).

In verse 14 Paul indicates that the fact of the Resurrection shows the importance of the body. Meats and the belly are to be destroyed. This present mortal body will be sufficiently similar to the resurrection body to demand reverence for its present state (15:42–50). Sexual immorality is an act of the whole person. Such an act defiles the body that the Lord will raise up. Such perversion cannot be tolerated.

In verses 15–17 Paul shows that the use of the body in adultery takes it away from its proper Lord. The church in its totality is the body of Christ, the organism with which He carries out His will on earth. Such a precious instrument must not be taken from the Lord and given to a harlot. This deed would involve a revolt against God and an act of self-debasement.

How unspeakably horrible! In verse 16 Paul refers to Genesis 2:24 to show that one joined by sexual relations with a harlot becomes one with her. Sexual union brings "a psychosomatic union, not a merely physical one" (Bruce). Sexual union engages and expresses the entire personality in a demonstration of self-commitment. One of God's saints must not make such a commitment to a harlot. The intention of the Lord is that one united with Him be one spirit (v. 17). Union with Christ is made possible by faith and personal surrender of the personality that He has purchased. It is a real union, a spiritual union, and it demands an exclusive commitment. There is no room for competition from a harlot.

Paul's conclusions to the entire discussion are summarized in verses 18–20. Paul demands in verse 18 that evasive action be taken to avoid fornication. In Corinth such a mindset would be vital. He then contrasts the effects of fornication with other sins such as drunkenness and gluttony. Those sins do affect the body, but only in excess. Fornication is sinful in itself. The effects of gluttony and drunkenness can in large measure be remedied by abstinence, but the effect of fornication is much deeper. In fornication man sins against his inner personality. This is what Paul means by the second reference to "body" in verse 18. It should cause little wonder that the sexually promiscuous person actually destroys his own personality. Such a result is inherent in the nature of the sin. Paul's question in verse 19 seems to suggest that the Corinthians may have forgotten that they were God's. In 3:16 the Christian community at Corinth was called God's temple, and here the body of the individual believer is seen as the sacred shrine of God's Spirit. Because of this gift of the Spirit the Christian no longer has the right to handle his body at will. God has taken possession of the body by the Holy Spirit, and such is His right. The statements of verse 20 establish God's rights to our bodies because of the price paid by Christ at Calvary. The imagery that Paul uses here is the process whereby a slave saves the price of his freedom, deposits it into the treasury of a pagan temple, and is then seen as purchased by the god. Technically he was the slave of the god, but before men he was free. Christians are free before men, for "everything is permissible" for them. They are God's slaves, for He has purchased them as His own. They are to use their bodies for the glory of God. Glorifying God calls for more than mere humanitarian gestures or respectable morality. To glorify God seeks His honor as the highest goal.

Throughout this section Paul shows a healthy respect for the human body. He would never find a basis for agreement with the frequently quoted modern adage that "man is what he eats." Godet notes that "contempt of the body goes side by side with abuse of the body, while respect for the body will always be the best means of ruling it."

Paul has also provided principles by which believers can use their bodies wisely:

1. Avoid what is not profitable or useful (v. 12a). Here Christian freedom is limited by one's regard for others.

2. Avoid what will enslave (v. 12b). Here Christian freedom is limited by regard for oneself.

3. Avoid what does not promote the dignity and destiny of the body (vv. 13–20). Paul points out that the body is for the Lord's service (v. 13) and is destined for resurrection (v. 14). The body is a member of Christ (v. 15) and is the temple of the Holy Spirit (v. 19). It is thus to be used as an instrument for glorifying God (v. 20).

For Further Study

1. Read the article on "Church" in *The Zondervan Pictorial Bible Dictionary*.

2. Does your church impose discipline on errant church members? For what types of actions does your church impose this discipline?

3. List suggestions of actions that churches could take to encourage a higher standard of commitment among their members.

4. Read 5:9–13 and then list methods by which you can relate more effectively to non-Christians who have a different lifestyle from you.

5. Read 6:1–8 and then consider what action you might take concerning a past due debt owed you by a Christian. Use also suggestions from other passages of Scripture as they come to mind.

6. After reading 6:12–20 list principles that could guide you in deciding whether you should participate in activities that might be questionable for Christians.

Chapter 4

Questions About Marriage
(1 Corinthians 7:1–40)

The preceding portion of the epistle (certainly 1:10–4:21 and probably chapters 5 and 6 as well) has dealt with matters brought to Paul's attention by "Chloe's people." Beginning with chapter 7 the discussion takes a new turn. The reference to "the matters you wrote about" (v. 1) suggests that the Corinthian church (note the plural "you") had sent a letter of inquiry to Paul, perhaps by Stephanas, Fortunatus, and Achaicus (16:17). (One should take note of the recurrence of the phrases "now for" and "now about" [Gr., *peri de*], used by the apostle to introduce the various topics mentioned in the letter that he had received from the church [cf. 7:1, marriage and divorce; 7:25, virginity; 8:1, food offered to idols; 12:1, spiritual gifts; 16:1, the collection for Jerusalem; 16:12, Apollos].) It is possible that other matters discussed in chapters 7 through 16, not introduced by the phrase "now for" or "now about" are responses to questions raised by the Corinthians in their letter. Some of the subjects discussed were purely local and of only temporary interest, but the principles enunciated by the apostle in dealing with them are of abiding significance.

Chapter 7 relates to a cluster of questions, all having to do in some way with marriage. It is easy to misunderstand Paul's teachings here, and he has accordingly been severely criticized for what some think is a low view of marriage. Several things should therefore be kept in mind. First, he was not writing a general treatise on marriage but was answering specific questions put to him by the Corinthians. (We cannot always be sure of the exact content of the question being answered. Reading the chapter with this handicap, one feels somewhat as though he were listening to one side of a telephone conversation: he hears all the answers and responses but can only guess what was asked or said on the other end of the line.) Some aspects of marriage that the apostle considered important (cf. Eph. 5:22–33) are not touched on here simply because the Corinthians had not asked for his advice on these. Second, one must bear in mind that the

Corinthians' questions probably reflected controversy within the church. Paul therefore was responding to erroneous views of marriage that were held by various segments of the church. Some (probably those with Jewish background) apparently thought of marriage as an absolute duty. Others (perhaps influenced by certain forms of Greek philosophy) regarded the marriage state as morally inferior to the celibate life. Still others seem to have held that when one became a Christian all existing social relationships, including marriage, ceased to be binding. Finally, it is to be observed that in writing this chapter Paul was aware of certain unusual conditions that were local and temporary (cf. vv. 2 and 26, which speak respectively of the prevailing sexual pressures of life in Corinth and of a current emergency designated by the apostle as "the present crisis"). His advice was colored by these considerations.

The following division of material isolates the various emphases of the passage: verses 1–9, a statement of general principles that may be thought of as *advice for all;* verses 10–24, *advice for the married* on the question whether divorce is permissible; verses 25–35, *advice to the unmarried* on whether they should marry or remain single; verses 36–38, *advice to parents/guardians* concerning their virgin daughters; and verses 39 and 40, *advice with respect to widows* on the question of remarriage. All of this resolves itself into two broad questions: whether the unmarried are to marry, and whether the married are to continue to live together.

A. Advice to All: A Statement of General Principles (7:1–9)

In ancient times there was a widespread inclination to regard celibacy as preferable to marriage. It would seem that at least some in the Corinthian church shared this view and argued that it was morally wrong for Christians to marry. In the passage before us Paul appears to be addressing this attitude. At least two questions seem to underlie the discussion: (1) Is it permissible for Christians to marry? (2) Are married couples to continue normal sexual relations after becoming Christians? In treating these matters Paul sets forth certain basic principles on which the remainder of the chapter rests.

1. *Marriage is not obligatory, but it is the norm* (7:1–2)

Verse 1: It is debated how verse 1b should be punctuated. Most versions (among them KJV, ASV, RSV, NIV, NEB) read it as an express teaching of Paul; others (correctly, we think) place it in quotation marks, understanding it to be a statement extracted from the Corinthians' letter to Paul. Moffatt, for example, has: "It is indeed 'an excellent thing for a man to have no intercourse with a woman'." Bruce brings out the meaning in paraphrase: "'It is a good thing,' some of you say, 'for a man to have nothing to do with a woman'" (*The Letters of Paul*).

"Good" (Gr., *kalon*), a word of such broad meaning that its context must always determine the exact definition, here means "all right," "honorable," "commendable" (cf. the colloquial "okay"). Robertson and Plummer interpret it here as having the sense of "laudable." Moffatt uses the word "excellent." It does not mean "better"; nor does it imply that the married state is not also good.

"Man" is generic (Gr., *anthropos;* not *anēr,* "husband"), practically equivalent to the indefinite pronoun "one." "To marry" ("to touch" KJV) implies sexual intercourse, though here it includes the whole idea of marriage. It therefore means not to have a woman in marriage, to be celibate, to remain unmarried. The TCNT reads: "It would be well for a man to remain single."

Verse 2 qualifies the meaning of the preceding statement. Though it is all right not to marry, the general rule is that "each man should have his own wife" and "each woman her own husband," because of "immorality." We are not to conclude that Paul thought this to be the only reason for marriage; however, he did consider it an important reason. "Immorality" is a translation of the most general word in Greek for illicit sexual relations. Some versions render it "fornication" (KJV). In the Greek it is plural, which calls attention to the prevalence of acts of immorality in first-century Corinth. The statement of the verse is to be interpreted as a command, not merely as a permission granted (as the English "let" [KJV, ASV] might suggest). "Each" appears to be absolute, but in light of what is said in verse 9 we should interpret it as limited to persons who could not control their sexual desires.

2. Marriage is to be with one person (7:2)

Paul says the relation is monogamous, not polygamous. This is suggested by "each man . . . his own wife," "each woman her own husband" (v. 2). The teaching on monogamy, though brought in "only incidentally," was "by no means unnecessary at this time, when polygamy was recklessly encouraged by the Jewish rabbis" (Lightfoot).

3. Marriage involves physical obligations binding on both husband and wife (7:3–5)

The KJV speaks of husband and wife rendering "due benevolence" (Gr., *opheilomenēn eunoian,* good will that is owed) to one another, but the better Greek text uses a word that simply means debt, what is owed (*opheilēn*). In this context it means "marital duty" (NIV), "conjugal rights"

(RSV). The thought is that neither partner in marriage is free to withhold sexual relations from the other (v. 3); married persons do not have exclusive authority over their own bodies[1] (v. 4). Each is the other's possession, their union being of such nature that they form a single complex personality; they are "one flesh" (cf. 6:16). As Robertson and Plummer affirm, "in wedlock separate ownership of the person ceases." In light of this, for one partner to withhold sexual relations from the other is to defraud (i.e., cheat, steal from; cf. 6:7–8 for the same Greek word) the mate (v. 5). "Defraud" is the word used in the ASV. The NIV has "deprived."

Any departure from normal sexual relations within marriage must be by mutual consent and agreement, for a limited time, and for a specific purpose ("so that you may devote yourselves to prayer")[2]. When this period of special communion with God is completed, husband and wife are to resume normal sexual relations ("come together again"), being mindful of the danger of sexual immorality arising from a lack of self-control (v. 5).

"Deprive" (NIV) simply suggests withholding. However, the Greek word has a connotation of robbing or cheating. The Greek uses a present tense, which with the negative may be rendered "stop depriving (robbing), etc." This is perhaps an indication that some of the Corinthian Christians were indeed depriving their marriage partners of their conjugal rights—a reflection of the ascetic tendencies mentioned above.

The marital rights and duties of husbands and wives are reciprocal and equal. This is brought out by the striking parallelism of verses 3 and 4. Each right/duty expressed for one member of the marriage union is matched by an almost exact restatement of that right/duty for the other member. By using the same expressions in reference to both husband and wife Paul affirms equality between the sexes, "thus correcting Jewish and Gentile ideas about women" (Robertson and Plummer).

4. *To marry or not to marry is a matter of choice for the individual* (7:6)

"I say this as a concession [permission, allowance], not as a command." The demonstrative "this" may refer to the statement of verse 2 or to the

---

[1]The word "body" may stand here for the whole person (cf. ch. 6; Rom. 12:1). Norlie's rendering expresses this: "The wife does not have sole authority over her own person, for she belongs to her husband. . . ." C. B. Williams, on the other hand, appears to confine the word to its more common meaning: "The wife does not have the right to do as she pleases with her own body; the husband has his right to it . . . " (cf. NEB).

[2]The KJV translates from a Greek text that includes the words "and fasting," but the better Greek text does not contain these words.

entire teaching of verses 2–5. Either way, the point is that though marriage is desirable, according to God's plan, and natural for most people, it is not mandatory.[3] God has given no command that reads "Thou shalt marry." Whether one marries is not a question of right or wrong, obedience or disobedience; either marital state is permissible. The word translated "concession" suggests an allowance made out of regard for circumstances and temperament.

5. *The decision about marriage should be made in light of one's special gift from God* (7:7–9)

In verse 7 Paul indicates that his preference (under the circumstances alluded to several times in the remainder of the chapter) is for the celibate life[4]—a statement in harmony with the thought of verse 1. But he admits that his own personal feeling is not decisive. The all-important consideration is whether one has the grace-gift (Gr., *charisma*) of continence (self-control), and Paul recognizes that all do not have this special gift.[5]

Verses 8 and 9 restate and enforce this principle. Verse 9 contains a translation of a Greek expression that literally means "cannot hold themselves in," that is, cannot control themselves. To "burn with passion" probably means to be consumed with uncontrollable desire. Bruce, however, suggests that the Greek, which literally means "to burn," could mean "to burn in Gehenna because of falling into fornication (in thought if not in action)."

B. Advice for the Married: Is Divorce Permissible? (7:10–24)

This unit of material falls naturally into three parts: verses 10–11, dealing with marriages in which both husband and wife are believers; verses 12–16, dealing with mixed marriages—one partner a believer, the

---

[3]Barrett prefers to understand all of verse 5 as the antecedent of "this." He expresses the thought of verses 5 and 6 as follows: "You should (Paul's advice runs) not rob one another of your rights, but I will make this concession to the ascetics among you (whose voice is heard in verse 1): If husband and wife both wish, they may agree not to cohabit for a short time, in order to give themselves without distraction to prayer. But note: this is concession, not command, and if you do practice abstinence in this way it must be for a limited time, and with a view to returning to each other."

[4]We have no way of knowing for sure whether Paul was ever married. There are three possibilities: (1) that he had always been single (the view perhaps most widely held), (2) that he was a widower, or (3) that he had been married and that his wife left him (at the time of his conversion? cf. Phil. 3:8).

[5]It is a question whether verse 7a has reference to Paul's singleness or to his possession of the gift that made that life possible. Robertson and Plummer opt for the latter interpretation, adding that "it does not follow that every man who has this gift is bound to live a life of celibacy" (p. 136).

other a pagan; verses 17–24, stating the principle underlying Paul's advice.

1. Is divorce permissible in marriages in which both partners are believers? (7:10–11)

Apparently there were some in Corinth who felt that conversion to Christ necessitated the disruption of all social relationships (cf. vv. 17–24), including marriage. These therefore felt they should separate from their Christian spouses and live celibate lives. In the present passage the apostle reminds them of the explicit command of Christ (cf. Matt. 5:32; 19:9; Mark 10:9; Luke 16:18), which forbids divorce, and added that should they separate (contrary to the Lord's command) remarriage is prohibited. Under such circumstances the believer has only two options: be reconciled to the estranged husband/wife or remain unmarried. The wording of the passage is carefully balanced so as to suggest that the marriage tie is equally binding on husband and wife.[6]

Verse 10: "I give this command" is the translation of a word that has a strong connotation of authority, being used in secular Greek of a military command. In saying "not I, but the Lord" the apostle affirms that Christ Himself had legislated for His people on this issue and Paul needs only to repeat His teaching. "Separate" (lit., "be separated"), used in verses 10 and 11 in reference to the wife, in this context means "to divorce" (Arndt and Gingrich). Though passive, the Greek term may be reflexive, "separate herself," suggesting that the divorce is the wife's act, not her husband's. Findlay comments that "Christianity had powerfully stirred the feminine mind at Corinth (xi. 5, xiv. 34)," adding that "In some cases ascetic aversion caused the wife to separate."

Verse 11: The first part of verse 11 ("But . . . husband") should be enclosed in parentheses (cf. ASV, RSV, and other modern translations). The two alternatives—to remain unmarried or else be reconciled to the mate—apparently leave no room for the "exception clause" of Matthew 5:32 and 19:9, and this has occasioned no small debate among interpreters. Some conjecture that the exception clause was not known to Paul, perhaps because it had not been made by Christ but was added later. (1 Corinthians is generally thought to have been written before the Gospel according to Matthew.) It seems better to suppose that Paul is describing

---

[6]It is somewhat surprising that the apostle mentions first the case of a woman divorcing the husband. Robertson and Plummer think this "indicates that such a thing had actually occurred or was mentioned in their letter as likely to occur. Women may have raised the question."

the case of a woman who divorces her husband *for an insufficient reason*. In so doing she violates the command of Christ, for *no adultery is involved*. She therefore ought to be reconciled to her husband; if she refuses to do this, let her at least remain unmarried. The exception clause of Matthew 5:32 and 19:9 is unmentioned by the apostle, not because he was unaware of it, but because it was not applicable to the situation at hand.

Having spoken to the case of a wife separating herself from her husband (vv. 10b, 11a), Paul now adds that "a husband must not divorce [lit., put away] his wife." The wife is enjoined not to separate herself (Gr., *choristhēnai*) from her husband; the husband is charged not to put away (Gr., *aphienai*) his wife. Robertson and Plummer explain that the change in terms is related to the social customs of the first century: "The home is his [the husband's]: she [the wife] can leave it, but he sends her away from it."

Though it is not expressly stated, the balanced parallelism of verses 10 and 11 suggests that Paul expected of the husband who put away his wife exactly what he expected of the wife who separated herself from her husband: either to be reconciled to the spouse or to remain unmarried.

2. *Is divorce permissible in marriages in which one partner is a believer and the other an unbeliever?* (7:12–16)

This is a more complex situation than that described in verses 10 and 11. The marriage in question was probably one that was entered into while both partners were unbelievers (pagans).[7] Some time subsequent to the forming of the union one spouse became a Christian and the other remained a pagan. Under these conditions was the believer to continue in the marriage state with an unbeliever? Was the Christian husband or wife compelled to live with a pagan mate?

Christ left no explicit answer to this question, but Paul gives his own inspired counsel. (This is the force of the introductory statement in verse 12: "To the rest I say this [I, not the Lord]." This does not mean that the apostle regards his words as having no authority, or less authority than the statements of verses 10 and 11. He simply means that on this matter he cannot quote a word from the teaching of the Lord. Christ's ministry was confined almost exclusively to the Jewish nation, and He apparently had no occasion to deal with mixed marriages involving His people and pagans.) The teaching of the passage is that conversion to Christ does not

---

[7]It is possible that some Christians had married unbelievers (cf. v. 39).

justify divorcing one's mate, nor does the continuing unbelief of that mate constitute a ground for divorce.

Two supposed cases of mixed marriages are considered, the one of an unbeliever willing to continue living with a believing mate (vv. 12–14), the other of an unbeliever refusing to continue living with the Christian spouse (vv. 15–16).

a) *The case of a Christian married to an unbeliever who is willing to continue the marriage relationship* (7:12–14)

Paul's response to this situation is that so long as the unbeliever is willing to continue in the marriage relationship, the Christian is not to take the initiative in severing the union.

The only real problem in this unit is that raised by verse 14: "For the unbelieving husband has been sanctified through his wife, and the unbelieving wife has been sanctified through her believing husband. Otherwise your children would be unclean, but as it is they are holy." It is perhaps easier to say what this verse does *not* mean than it is to explain what it does mean. It obviously does not mean that a Christian's family will be saved by virtue of the Christian's faith. Such a teaching would contradict the plain and unambiguous statements of Paul about salvation and would run counter to the whole tenor of Scripture.

In the first part of the verse, which deals with the husband/wife relationship, the crux of the problem is in the expression "has been sanctified." The NEB interprets it to mean that "the heathen husband now *belongs to God* through his Christian wife . . . " (italics ours). *The Living Bible* expresses it as follows: "For perhaps the husband who isn't a Christian may become a Christian with the help of his Christian wife. . . ." The TCNT has: "For, through the wife, the husband who is an unbeliever has become associated with Christ's people. . . ." Not one of these translations is satisfactory.

In Paul "sanctified" is a term that describes Christians. However, since the persons described in this verse as "sanctified" are clearly identified as unbelievers standing outside the realm of salvation (v. 16), the term must be used here in a sense different from that ordinarily found in Paul's writings. Perhaps the general idea is that the marriage *relationship* is hallowed in spite of the fact that one partner is an unbeliever. Therefore, believers married to unbelievers must not think that they will be defiled by the sexual intercourse of marriage or that the children born of that union will be unclean (illegitimate). "The piety of the one has more effect in sanctifying the marriage than the impiety of the other in polluting it" (Calvin).

b) *The case of a Christian married to an unbeliever who refuses to continue the marriage relationship* (7:15–16)

Paul's decision on this matter is that if an unbeliever insists on severing the marriage tie, the believer is to acquiesce. Three reasons are given for pursuing this course: First, the believer is not in bondage under such circumstances (v. 15b). "The implication," writes Bruce, "is that the believer in such a case was in a state of what amounted to widowhood." This being so, it would seem that the deserted/repudiated partner is free to remarry.[8] Second, the Christian has been called—the reference is to the call to conversion—in peace (v. 15a). To cling to a marriage which one partner is determined to end would lead to nothing but frustration and strife. Third, the possibility of an unhappy, strife-torn marriage resulting in the unbeliever's conversion is uncertain at best (v. 16). To use Morris's words, "Paul's meaning is that marriage is not to be regarded simply as an instrument of evangelism."[9] *The Living Bible* conveys the sense: "For after all, there is no assurance to you wives that your husbands will be saved if they stay. . . ."

3. *The principle involved in Paul's advice* (7:17–24)

This paragraph is not a digression having primary reference to circumcision and slavery, as some have supposed, but is closely related to the overall discussion of marriage. As Robertson and Plummer explain, it

---

[8]Edwards lists three reasons in favor of this view: "(1) No other explanation does justice to the words 'is not enslaved;'. . . . (2) Equity seems to require that at least a person that has not the power of continence should not be precluded from marrying in a case of final desertion. . . . (3) If the desertion is absolute and final, the marriage is *de facto* dissolved. But why is it permitted to a widower to contract a second marriage, if not because death annuls a marriage *de facto?* By parity of reason may we not argue that final desertion, as it brings the union to an end actually, leaves the deserted believer free to marry another?"

[9]In fairness it should be observed that verse 16 may be interpreted in a manner exactly opposite to that proposed above. We understand the verse to express *doubt* about the future conversion of the unbelieving spouse. Others take it to express *hope* that he/she will be converted. We take the verse as the expression of a reason for letting the unbeliever depart if he/she is determined to do so. Others see it as a reason for clinging to the marriage even if one's partner wants to give it up. Bruce, who favors the latter interpretation, observes that in the Old Testament the phrase "Who knows whether . . . ?" "is used in the hopeful sense of 'perhaps'" and adds that the similar phrase used twice in verse 16 ("how knowest thou . . . ?") may have that same sense. "The meaning would then be: 'Do not dissolve your marriage with the unbelieving partner who is willing to remain; perhaps you will be his (her) salvation.'" Barrett follows a similar line of reasoning. The NEB expresses it: "Think of it: as a wife you may be your husband's salvation. . . ."

states the general principle that determines much of the counsel given by Paul throughout this chapter about marriage.

The principle, which is stated in verses 17, 20, and 24, has been variously designated as the principle of peace, of contentment, or of the status quo. It may be summed up as follows: Though conversion to Christ effects radical changes in the moral and spiritual life, it does not necessitate a complete alteration of status; indeed, it is usually best to abide in the condition in which one receives the call to be a Christian. This means that the marriage relationship should not be lightly dissolved (as we saw in vv. 10–16). If one is unmarried, he/she should be content to remain so (which is the burden of vv. 25ff.).

a) First statement of the principle (7:17)

"Nevertheless, each one should retain the place in life that the Lord assigned to him, and to which God has called him." The word translated "assigned" means to apportion to one his share in something. The "something" that has been apportioned to each is not stated. However, the context suggests that the reference is to what the NIV calls one's "place in life."

In verse 17b Paul affirms that he ordains or "lays down" this principle in all the churches. This is the translation of a Greek word having a military connotation.

Paul's insistence on this "rule" was wise. Christianity taught the equality of all people in Christ, and new converts were probably prone to transfer this sense of equality to all the relationships of life. But to alter the gospel into a mere instrument of social change would have been fatal to the Christian mission. "The gospel will work and has worked its social reformations, but it has done so in the manner of leaven rather than by revolution" (Fisher).

b) First application of the principle (7:18–19)

This principle is illustrated by (and applied to) circumcision and slavery, two of the chief social distinctions of the day. Concerning the former, discussed in verses 18 and 19, Paul argues that the circumcised believer did not need to remove the mark of his circumcision (v. 18a) nor should the uncircumcised believer submit to the rite (v. 18b). In itself the presence or the absence of circumcision is a matter of religious indifference (v. 19a); it has no significance for the living of the Christian life. What is supremely important is the keeping of God's commandments (cf. Gal. 5:6;

6:15 for similar statements).[10] To "keep" God's commandment is to obey them.

c) Second statement of the principle (7:20)

This is given in terms only slightly different from those used in verse 17. "Situation in life" is a correct interpretation of the Greek text, though the word used there is literally "calling."

d) Second application of the principle (7:21–23)

In verses 21–23 Paul relates this principle to slavery. He spoke first to those who had become Christians while in bondage. They were urged not to chafe at their state in life but to be content in it (v. 21a),[11] remembering that they had experienced in Christ a spiritual liberation that had made them the Lord's freedmen (v. 22a).

Verses 22b and 23 are addressed to those who were free. They were reminded that although they were free from bondage to men, they were not free in reference to Christ. Being a Christian means that one has surrendered to the lordship of Christ—thus becoming His "slave."

e) Third statement of the principle (7:24)

One is to remain "with God" in the state in which he was called (v. 24). Whatever that condition may have been—circumcision or uncircumcision, slavery or freedom—it is now transformed by the fact that the believer is *responsible to God*. The preposition probably means "by the side of" or "on the side of." It suggests that our attachment is to God.

C. Advice for the Unmarried: Should They Marry or Remain Single? (7:25–35)

Earlier in the chapter (vv. 8,9) Paul touched briefly on the situation of those who were unmarried. Here he discusses the matter in much greater detail. The earlier passage was addressed to "the unmarried and widows,"

---

[10]A Jew might argue that circumcision is itself one of God's commandments. Paul, however, was identifying the commandments of God with the law of Christ (cf. 1 Cor. 9:20f.; Gal. 6:2). Keeping God's coi n̄ ndments therefore "means obedience to the will of God as declared in his Son" (Barrett).

[11]The latter half of verse 21 is so tersely stated in Greek that it may legitimately be interpreted and translated in two very different ways. The RSV represents one: "But if you can gain your freedom, avail yourself of the opportunity." The other interpretation, the exact opposite of that expressed in RSV, is given in Barrett's translation: "but even though you should be able to become free, put up rather with your present status."

the first term being a very broad one including all not bound by the ties of marriage, the latter calling special attention to a group of unmarried persons who were perhaps more vulnerable and consequently tempted strongly to remarry. In the present passage the apostle was thinking mainly of virgins (v. 25), though brief reference is made to unmarried men (v. 32) and to women previously married (v. 34).

Although the essential meaning of the passage before us is clear, it does present several exegetical difficulties. Our treatment of the text may best be presented under two heads, having to do with (1) the nature (v. 25) and (2) the substance (vv. 26–35) of Paul's instructions.

1. The nature of Paul's instructions (7:25)

First, all that is written in this paragraph was apparently a response to a question raised by the Corinthians in their letter to Paul. This is suggested by the opening phrase of verse 25. (See the discussion at the beginning of this chapter.) Second, the apostle explains that he has no direct teaching of the Lord that he can quote on the question at hand. This is the force of "I have no command from the Lord" (cf. vv. 10, 12). Third, what he says in this unit is in the nature of advice—a judgment, an opinion.[12] Bruce remarks that "Paul's reluctance to impose rules in a situation where he probably had strong feelings about the proper course to follow illustrates the strength of his libertarian principles." Fourth, Paul hastens to add that his advice is trustworthy: he speaks as "one who by the Lord's mercy is trustworthy." Edwards expresses the meaning thus: "I give my advice, not frivolously or as a man wise in this world, but with all the faithfulness and sincerity of one that has had the grace of salvation and apostleship." The Corinthians should therefore take his advice seriously.

2. The substance of Paul's instructions (7:26–35)

It would be a mistake to apply to Christians of every generation and place the advice given to the Corinthians in this passage. Two enigmatic phrases point up the fact that the Corinthian Christians were living in

---

[12]Edwards' comment is worthy of note: "Whatever Christ says in reference to practice is a command, which men disobey at their peril. But the Apostles, though they may often have authority to command, may also be unable on occasion to arrive at a decision and, therefore, rest content with the expression of an opinion, which Christians may, if they so judge, lay aside. The present passage is an instance of this. The Spirit's enlightenment does not lead the Apostle to a decision. He gives his advice, therefore, and imposes no command."

especially trying times. Verse 26 speaks of some particular "distress"[13] they were experiencing. (The Greek suggests a distress that has begun and is now present.) We do not know what this was, but the reference probably is to some unusually difficult conditions through which the Corinthians were at that time passing. This makes the advice given earlier (vv. 17–24) about remaining in one's existing state of life even more appropriate. "The apostle writes to the Corinthians as he would do to an army about to enter on a most unequal conflict in an enemy's country, and for a protracted period" (Hodge). Another phrase that colors the advice given here is in verse 29: "the time is short." This has been interpreted as a reference to approaching death, to the return of Christ, and to the transitoriness of life. But it is best to see the words as an allusion to the "crisis" mentioned in verse 26. In saying that "the time is short" Paul probably meant that a crisis—perhaps a storm of persecution—was approaching. Conditions were already bad, but they were going to get worse—soon. The general sense is: "time is running out."

Paul's advice moves along two lines. First, because of the present distress he thought it best for believers in Corinth not to change their marital state: "it is good for you to remain as you are" (v. 26). Those who were married were not to dissolve the marriage, but were to accept patiently the responsibilities attending married life (v. 27a); those who were not married were to be content to remain so (v. 27b). Verse 28 emphasizes again that the apostle was only giving advice. To marry or not to marry was not a matter of right or wrong but of expediency and personal choice. If the unmarried Christians of Corinth were to ignore Paul's advice they would not thereby sin (v. 28a). Paul, however, was convinced that marriage under the conditions of life in Corinth would increase their troubles, and he wanted to spare them the anxiety and agony that family responsibilities inevitably bring in times of trouble (v. 28b). Robertson and Plummer quote Bacon as saying that "children sweeten labours, but they make misfortunes more bitter."

Second, because "the time is short"—that is, a crisis will soon come—the Corinthian Christians needed to cultivate a certain detachment from the present world order (vv. 29–31). The Greek word for "mean" (v. 29) is *phēmi*, not the more common *legō*. It probably gives a connotation of special solemnity to the statements that follow. The sense is: "But, though I counsel none to change their state, I do counsel all to change *their attitude* toward all earthly things" (Robertson and Plummer).

---

[13]The Greek word basically means "necessity," but frequently was used in the postclassical period in the sense of distress or calamity.

Bruce calls attention to the fourfold "as if" of verses 29–31 and comments that this repeated phrase emphasizes that "the Christian should as far as possible live in this age *as though* the age to come were already here, regulating life by its values and not by those current among 'the sons of this age.' The values of this age are transient and relative; those of the age to come are permanent and absolute."

Remembering then how temporary all of their earthly surroundings were, the Corinthian Christians were to avoid becoming engrossed in them. Mention is made of marriage (v. 29), the emotions of sorrow and joy (v. 30a), the buying and possessing of goods (v. 30b), and the use of the world (i.e., all its resources and opportunities).[14]

Third, the Corinthian Christians were to follow the course that would enable them to serve God with a minimum of distraction (vv. 32–35). Care should be taken not to interpret verse 34 as teaching that the unmarried woman is morally more pure than the married woman. That this is not the meaning is clear from the fact that Paul has already said that marriage is not a sin (v. 28). The essence of Paul's teaching here is that the unmarried person is less encumbered and therefore more free to render certain types of service to God than is the married person.[15]

Paul's concern was that his readers should be "free from concern [anxieties]" (v. 32); he was speaking for their benefit or advantage (v. 35a), not at all wanting to put a noose ("restraint," NASB) about them and deprive them of liberty to marry (v. 35b).

---

[14]These verses contain several profound implications. For example, the institution of marriage, though established by divine appointment, belongs to the temporal order, and with the passing of that order marriage will also pass away (cf. Mark 12:25). Paul's advice to the Corinthians is to prepare for the eternal order now—"not by divorcing [their wives], or ceasing to cohabit with [them] (still less, we may add, by ceasing to love [them] and enjoy [their] society . . .), but by recognizing that very soon their relationship will be on an entirely different basis" (Barrett).

Again, with respect to sorrow and joy, there is a distinctly Christian approach. Both have a place in the Christian life, for in Romans 12:15 Paul urges believers to rejoice with those who rejoice and weep with those who weep. The import of the present passage, however, is that "neither laughter nor tears is the last word," and Christians should not allow themselves "to be lost in either" (Barrett).

Finally, Christians may "use" the world but are forbidden to be absorbed in it—for the simple reason that all of its institutions—social, commercial, etc.—are transitory and temporary. "The fashion [the outward show, the present form] of the world is passing away" (v. 31).

[15]Some interpreters think the words "her aim is to be devoted to the Lord in both body and spirit" are a quotation from the Corinthians' letter to Paul and that they reflect a certain ascetic tendency on the part of some Corinthian Christians.

D. Advice for Parents: What Is Their Responsibility Toward Their Virgin Daughters in Reference to Marriage? (7:36–38)

The Greek of these verses is capable of being interpreted in several ways. The most critical question concerns the identity of the "man" and his "virgin" (vv. 36, 37, and 38). Related questions have to do with the meaning of the word translated "getting along in years" (v. 36b); whether this word is describing the man, or his virgin; and the meaning of the word rendered "marries" (v. 38). To see the various ways in which these questions have been answered, one should consult some of the versions of the New Testament. These reflect at least three principal lines of interpretation.

The NASB reads as follows:

> But if any man thinks that he is acting unbecomingly toward his virgin *daughter*, if she should be of full age, and if it must be so, let him do what he wishes, he does not sin; let them marry. But he who stands firm in his heart, being under no constraint, but has authority over his own will, and has decided this in his own heart, to keep his own virgin *daughter*, he will do well. So then both he who gives his own virgin *daughter* in marriage does well, and he who does not give her in marriage will do better.

This rendering interprets the "man" in the passage to be a father, "his virgin" to be his daughter. "Of full age"[16] is seen as a feminine adjective describing the daughter as being of marriageable age—or perhaps as past the bloom of youth. The girl apparently desires to marry but cannot without her father's permission. The father, having withheld permission for the reasons that led Paul in the preceding verses to suggest the desirability of the celibate life, is having misgivings ("thinks he is acting unbecomingly"). The "need" that seems to require her marriage (v. 36) may be the daughter's lack of continence—or perhaps her obvious unhappiness in not being married. Under these conditions Paul advises that the father may let her marry. In so doing, he commits no wrong. The decision is purely a matter of expediency and of circumstances. If, on the contrary, he refuses to give his daughter in marriage, he should have a definite conviction as to the wisdom of his course, should be sure there is no opposing necessity, and should possess the legal and moral right to exercise his restraint ("has authority over his own will").

Paul's personal feeling was that under the conditions of life in Corinth it

---

[16]The Greek word (*hyperakmos*) means "beyond (*hyper*) the highest point" (*akmos;* cf. English "acme"). As the meaning of *hyperakmos* Morris suggests "if she passes the stage of being fully developed." He cites Plato as saying that a woman was at her prime (*akmē*) at age twenty.

would be better for the father to keep his virgin daughter from marriage. Nevertheless, "he that giveth his virgin *daughter* in marriage doeth well" also.

The understanding of the passage reflected in the NASB is found also in Weymouth, *Jerusalem Bible*, Edwards, Robertson and Plummer, Morris, Lenski, and others. The KJV, though not as interpretive as the NASB, probably represents the same view.

A second interpretation sees the "man" and "his virgin" as a man and woman who have entered upon a "spiritual marriage"; that is, they live together but do not have sexual relations. This interpretation is expressed by NEB:

> But if a man has a partner in celibacy and feels that he is not behaving properly towards her, if, that is, his instincts are too strong for him, and something must be done, he may do as he pleases; there is nothing wrong in it; let them marry. But if a man is steadfast in his purpose, being under no compulsion, and has complete control of his own choice; and if he has decided in his own mind to preserve his partner in her virginity, he will do well. Thus, he who marries his partner does well, and he who does not will do better.

There are three principal objections to this view of the passage: (1) It runs counter to the clear teaching of verse 5, where the withholding of sexual relations within marriage is regarded as an act of fraud. (2) There is no evidence that the custom of "spiritual" marriages was practiced before the end of the second century. (3) The interpretation of the Greek word that lies behind "marries" (v. 38) is unnatural. Robertson and Plummer affirm that it means "*give* in marriage" everywhere in the New Testament, never "marry." This, they say, is the "decisive" argument against this interpretation.

The third interpretation takes the "man" and "his virgin" to be an engaged couple who have decided not to marry but are having misgivings about their decision. The TEV expresses this clearly:

> In the case of an engaged couple who have decided not to marry: if the man feels that he is not acting properly toward the girl; if his passions are too strong, and he feels that they ought to marry, then they should get married, as he wants to. There is no sin in this. But if a man, without being forced to do so, has firmly made up his mind not to marry; if he has his will under complete control, and has already decided in his own mind what to do— then he does well not to marry the girl. So the man who marries his girl does well, but the one who does not marry her will do even better.

Goodspeed, RSV, NIV, and others follow the same line of interpretation. C. K. Barrett, who is an advocate of this view of the passage, gives arguments in support of it.

E. Advice for Widows: Are They Free to Remarry? (7:39–40)

Since the case of widows is included in earlier general statements about the unmarried (vv. 8,34), it seems probable that Paul was here answering a specific question raised by the Corinthians in their letter. He treated the matter very briefly—so much so that some think verses 39 and 40 were added almost as an afterthought.

In these two verses we find the statement of a principle, the answer to a question, the addition of a limitation, the affirmation of an opinion, and a claim of authority. The *statement of principle* represents the divine ideal for marriage (cf. Matt. 19:5): "A woman is bound to her husband as long as he lives." Nothing is said about the husband's being bound, but doubtless this is also true. The form of Paul's statement was probably determined by the form of the question he was answering.

The *answer to their question* is that death severs the marriage bond: "if her husband dies (lit., "falls asleep," a euphemism for death; cf. 1 Thess. 4:13,14), she is free to marry anyone she wishes." There is nothing wrong or unseemly or unchristian in the remarriage of a widowed person. In fact, in 1 Timothy 5:14 Paul urges younger widows to remarry.

There is one *limitation* or qualification added to Paul's answer: The widow is free to marry whom she will, "but he must belong to the Lord." This is popularly interpreted to mean that the Christian widow is free to marry anyone she pleases, provided he is a believer (cf. Goodspeed's translation: "so long as he is a Christian"). The MLB expresses it more generally: "only in a Christian way." Robertson and Plummer interpret the phrase to mean "only as a member of Christ," which, they explain, "implies that she marries a Christian. To marry a heathen, especially in Corinth, would make loyalty to Christ very difficult." Barrett understands the Greek for "belong to the Lord" to mean "remembering only that she is a Christian."

Verse 40a gives *an opinion* or a judgment (Gr., *gnōmēn*): The widow will be "happier if she stays as she is," that is, in the unmarried state. It is to be observed that Paul does not say she will be morally or spiritually better, only that she will be happier. And this opinion must be understood in light of the peculiar circumstances of life in Corinth.

The chapter closes with *a claim of divine illumination* and inspiration: "I think[17] [regardless of what others may think or say] that I too have the Spirit of God" (v. 40b). Paul felt confident that his teaching in this chapter was not the expression of mere human prudence or of personal inclination. It came from the highest source and had the stamp of divine approval. We therefore do well to heed what he has written.

---

[17]Findlay calls "think" the "language of modesty, not misgiving."

For Further Study

1. Read Matthew 5:27–32; 19:3–12; Mark 10:2–12. Compare these passages with one another and with Paul's statements in 1 Corinthians 7:10–13.

2. Read the articles on "Marriage" and "Divorce" in *The Zondervan Pictorial Encyclopedia of the Bible*, or in some similar work.

3. Make a list of Paul's teachings about marriage in 1 Corinthians 7 and compare these with his teachings in Ephesians 5:22–33.

Chapter 5

The Limits of Liberty
(1 Corinthians 8:1–11:1)

A new subject is introduced by Paul at 8:1, suggested to the apostle in the letter written to him by the Corinthians. Although the larger problem that underlies the discussion of chapters 8–10 is Christian liberty (cf. 6:12–18; Rom. 14:1–15:13), the specific occasion for this section of material was the question whether Christians should eat meat that had been offered as a sacrifice to idols.

Godet points out that it was in sacrifice, which was at the center of the worship of all ancient religions, that all the important events of domestic and social life culminated. After the legs of the sacrifice (enclosed in fat) and the entrails had been burned on the altar, and after the priest had been given his share, what was left of the victim's flesh was returned to the family that offered the sacrifice. This consecrated meat was then eaten—either as part of a banquet in the pagan temple (or its precincts) or in the worshiper's home—or it was sold at the marketplace.

If the consecrated meat was used for a banquet—whether at the temple or in the worshiper's house—friends and relatives, among whom there might well be Christians, were invited. Christians would then find themselves confronted with the question of whether they should eat the idol meat. So also, when meats previously consecrated to a pagan deity were sold in the market, Christians might find themselves having to decide whether to purchase that meat.

References and allusions within this unit of material suggest that there were three aspects to the overall problem. First, a part of the passage relates to the question of whether Christians should eat consecrated meat in a temple setting (10:14–22). As observed above, the meat of pagan sacrifices often was served at a meal to which friends and relatives were invited, the temple functioning as a sort of banquet hall. Some, in the name of Christian liberty, affirmed that it was quite allowable for a Christian to participate in such a festive social occasion, perhaps using the adage that "everything is permissible for me" (cf. 6:12; 10:23). Others felt that such surroundings subjected one to the malign influence of demons.

Second, another reference in the passage brings up the question of purchasing meat at the market (10:25). As noted above, that portion of a sacrificial animal not given to the priest or consumed at the altar could be sold. Even the meat of animals slaughtered for the express purpose of being sold at the market was sometimes consecrated by a token offering to an idol. Therefore, when a Christian bought meat at the market there was always the possibility that it had had some association with idolatry. On this, as on the above-mentioned aspect of the problem, the opinions of the libertarians and the scrupulous differed.

Third, a part of the passage has to do with whether Christians should eat consecrated meat in a private home (10:27). The more scrupulous contended that this was not permissible for the Christian, since in their thinking the meat in question contracted defilement by its consecration to a pagan deity. For others, pagan deities represented no reality, were only imaginary beings, and meat offered on their altar remained ordinary meat, no different from any other.

Many readers might feel that all of this is irrelevant, but today, as in Paul's day, there are acts and practices as to whose moral qualities opinions of Christians differ. The conscience of some forbids certain courses of actions; the conscience of others, equally dedicated and sincere, allows them. To the latter they are matters of moral indifference; to the former they involve serious questions of right and wrong. The counsel offered by Paul in this passage, though he was dealing specifically with a question of little or no concern to Christians of the modern western world, provides great principles valuable to believers of every age as they face questions of conscience about which fellow Christians do not agree.

Paul was the champion of Christian liberty, the Galatian letter generally being recognized as his most direct and powerful exposition of this important theme. Some interpreters even see liberty as the motif of the entire epistle, with the first two chapters setting forth the "apostle of liberty," the next two "the gospel of liberty," and the final chapters describing the Christian life as a "life of liberty." The pivotal statement of Galatians may be the first verse of chapter 5: "It is for freedom that Christ has set us free. Stand firm, then, and do not let yourselves be burdened again by a yoke of slavery." Freedom, Paul teaches, is something to be cherished: the Christian should cling to it, stand firm in it.

Yet the Christian's freedom is not absolute. It has certain necessary limitations suggested by another statement in the Galatian letter: "You, my brothers, were called to be free. But do not use your freedom to indulge the sinful nature; rather, serve one another in love" (5:13). In the portion of 1 Corinthians that we are now approaching, Paul dealt with people who were abusing their liberty. Appropriately, therefore, he reminded them that liberty has its limits. The discussion falls into four parts, the first three showing that liberty is limited (1) by love for one's fellow believers (8:1–13), (2) by concern for the progress of the gospel (9:1–23), and (3) by solicitude for one's own spiritual well-being (9:24–10:22). There is a concluding summary in which practical suggestions are offered for the guidance of the Corinthians (10:23–11:1).

A. Liberty Limited by Love (8:1–13)

In his treatment of the question at hand Paul defends Christian freedom, but not without qualification. As Findlay puts it, "In theory Paul is for *freedom,* but in practice for great *restrictions* upon the use of *idolothyta* meat offered to an idol." Among these restrictions is that set forth in the present passage.

Chapter 8 contains three logical divisions: verses 1–3, verses 4–6, verses 7–13. In the first division Paul introduces the problem (v. 1a), and then contrasts two principles of action proposed as the solutions of the problem (vv. 1b–3). In the second and third divisions these two principles are discussed in greater depth, knowledge in verses 4–6, and love in verses 7–13.

1. The problem and its proposed solutions (8:1–3)

The problem is introduced by the phrase "Now about food sacrificed to idols" (v. 1a). We observed earlier that "Now about" is the formula used in this epistle to refer to questions raised in a letter the Corinthians had written to Paul. "Food sacrificed to idols" is the translation of a Greek term (*eidolothyta*) that was used only by Christians and Jews; pagans used a term (*hierothyta*) that meant devoted or sacrificed to a divinity. As noted above, the reference is to meat taken from the carcass of an animal offered on a pagan altar, and the problem was whether it was permissible for Christians to buy it, to eat it, or in any way participate in a festival where it was served.

Paul's response begins with a contrast between knowledge and love (vv. 1b–3), the former being the solution proposed by some of the Corinthians, the latter being the solution proposed by Paul. The RSV is probably correct in using quotation marks with the words "all of us possess knowledge,"[1] thereby indicating that Paul is quoting directly from the Corinthians' letter.[2] But even so, the apostle was obviously in essential

---

[1]"Knowledge" (Gr., *gnosis*) seems to have been a broad term including "Christian speculated theology in general" and "conclusions which required Christian social and moral behaviour" (Barrett).

[2]Alternatively, the "all" may be seen as a gentle rebuke to the pride of the Corinthian faction that made so much of their knowledge.

agreement with the statement. The context suggests that it was the more enlightened group (elsewhere designated as "the strong") who were acting on the basis of knowledge. The "knowledge" referred to is the knowledge that the gods represented by idols are nonexistent. What follows (vv. 1c–3) shows that such knowledge alone is an insufficient guide for Christian conduct. Love is the preferable principle. Three things are said that show this to be so. First, "knowledge puffs up" (that is, makes one conceited, arrogant, and proud), but "love builds up." The TCNT interprets it: "Knowledge breeds conceit, while love builds up character." Second, present knowledge is at best incomplete. "If any man thinks he already has knowledge, he does not truly know as he ought to know" (v. 2, Montgomery). Phillips renders it, ". . . he still has a lot to learn." Third, love has far-reaching implications. "But the man who loves God is known by God" (v. 3). The use of NIV as the basic text requires these changes. These words must not be interpreted to mean that one's love for God is a meritorious act rewarded by divine recognition. The thought is rather that love for God is a sign or evidence that one is known by Him. "Love" is not affection; it is devotion to God. To be "known" by God is to be one of His people.

2. Knowledge explained (8:4–6)

Verses 4–6 appear to restate the argument used by the libertarians (cf. NEB). The gist of it is that idols are nothing, and Christians are therefore free to eat food offered to them. Though Paul doubtless agreed with some of the things affirmed in these statements, verse 7 seems to require that not every detail of verses 4–6 be taken as expressing the judgment of Paul (cf. 10:19,20).

The central idea of the passage is that an idol amounts to nothing, has no real existence in the world. The literal rendering of verse 4 is, "There is no idol in the world." (NEB: "Of course, as you say, a false god has no existence in the real world.") The argument is that since there is only one God, an idol is a representation of a nonexistent god. When thought of in this manner, the idol itself may be said to have no real existence. From this affirmation it is to be inferred there is nothing really wrong with food offered to an idol. Buying it or eating it is a matter of moral indifference.

3. Love preferred (8:7–13)

The thought expressed in verses 4–6 was probably used by the libertarians at Corinth to argue that Christians are free to eat food offered to idols under any and all circumstances. However, the present passage (vv. 7–13), which picks up and develops the thought of verses 1–3, shows that mere knowledge is an inadequate guide. Love, not knowledge alone, must decide the Christian's course of conduct. The line of thought is this: There are some Christians who, because of lifelong involvement in idolatry, cannot rid themselves of the thought that consecrated food has been contaminated by its association with an idol. Their conscience being tender, they have a sense of guilt when they eat such food (v. 7b). Paul imagines the strong replying: "But food does not bring us near to God; we are no worse if we do not eat, and no better if we do" (v. 8). The eating of or abstaining from sacrificial food is a matter of moral indifference; neither will in itself enhance or jeopardize one's standing with God. Paul endorsed this view but cautioned "the strong" not to use their "freedom" (v. 9; lit., "authority," "right") in such a way as to do harm to "the weak" (those who need help, the overscrupulous, those with an inadequate understanding of Christian freedom). To inflict injury on a weak brother is to sin against Christ (vv. 10–12). All our conduct should therefore be tempered by considerate love (v. 13).

The passage mentions three painful consequences that befall "the weak" when they, by the unloving conduct of "the strong," are led to eat sacrificial food—something that they (because of their conditioning) consider wrong. First, their conscience (moral awareness), being weak, is defiled (v. 7). The weakness referred to is not an inability to *resist* evil, but to *distinguish* between things evil and things morally indifferent. The term may have been used contemptuously by "the strong" to ridicule their brothers. C. B. Williams employs the word "overscrupulous" in his translation.

For the conscience to be "defiled" is for it to be stained by a sense of guilt. "The weak" *feel* that they are defiled, and it is this *feeling* of defilement that makes the act wrong. Their conscience "is defiled, not by the partaking of polluted food, for food cannot pollute (Mark 7:18f.; Luke 11:41), but by the doing of something which the unenlightened conscience does not allow" (Robertson and Plummer).

Second, they are caused to stumble, that is, to sin (v. 9; cf. v. 13). Although the eating of sacrificial food was in itself an act morally indifferent, "the weak" thought otherwise, and for them to do deliberately that which they believed to be wrong was to rebel against God. "Everything that does not come from faith is sin" (Rom. 14:23). The imagery of "the stumbling block" is that of an obstacle being placed in a person's path, causing him to trip and to fall. (The danger referred to in v. 9 is enforced by v. 10, which should be compared with 10:19–20. In the present passage reclining at a table in an idol's temple is condemned because of its bad effect on others; in chapter 10 it is condemned on its own account.)

Third, they are brought down the path of destruction (v. 11). Bruce comments: "It is not the man's eternal perdition, but the stunting of his Christian life and usefulness by the 'wounding' of his conscience . . . that Paul has in mind." Mare writes similarly: "The stress is on weakening the faith and ruining the Christian life of the brother." To do this to a weak Christian is not only to sin against him but also to sin against Christ, for what is done to His people is counted as done to Him (Matt. 25:40,45; Mark 9:37,41; Luke 10:16; John 13:20; Acts 9:4).

It should be observed that Paul, though "strong" in conscience and gifted with "knowledge," comes down on the side of "the weak" in the matter under discussion—willing never to eat flesh if to do so would cause a brother to stumble (v. 13).

B. Liberty Limited by Concern for the Gospel (9:1–23)

Chapter 8 has shown that the Christian's liberty is limited by his love for the "weak" brother. Now, using his own experience as an example, Paul shows that liberty must sometimes be limited by our concern for the unimpeded progress of the gospel.

Some interpreters look on this passage as a parenthesis, having little or no connection with the matter of eating sacrificial meat. Bruce, for instance, speaks of it as a "sudden digression in which Paul turns aside to defend his apostleship before going on (in 10:1ff.) to deal with another aspect of the question about idol meat." Others have even theorized that this section is an insertion from another letter. There seems to be no need, however, to think of the passage as either an interpolation or a digression. Paul has been writing of those who insisted on their rights (cf. v. 9) to the detriment of their fellow believers, and he has condemned such actions. He now shows that what he urges on others he himself practices. He had let concern for the broader acceptance of the gospel regulate his own liberty, as a Christian and as an apostle. His personal conduct is thus represented as an instance of self-denying abstinence. In effect, he says, "I have not asked you to forego more rights than I forego myself. For the sake of the gospel and for the sake of those whom it benefits I surrender, not only what any Christian may claim, but what I can claim as an apostle." Verse 19 may be seen as expressing the heart of the apostle's testimony: "Though I am free and belong to no man, I make myself a slave to everyone, to win as many as possible."

In developing the thought of the passage Paul (1) establishes his rights (as a Christian, but mainly as an apostle, vv. 1–14), (2) reminds the readers of his willing renunciation of those rights in the interest of the gospel (vv. 15–18), and (3) points to other concessions that were made by him "for the sake of the gospel" (vv. 19–23).

1. *Paul's rights as an apostle* (9:1–14)

The rights of Paul's apostleship are the dominant idea of these verses, but he does not immediately expand on them. The passage begins with an implied assertion of liberty ("Am I not free?"[3]) followed by a similar claim to apostleship ("Am I not an apostle?"). The former question arises out of the foregoing discussion (ch. 8), and both are stated in a form that implies an affirmative answer. "Free" means that he was no longer bound by Mosaic restrictions in the matters under discussion in chapter 8. What is claimed is the freedom that belongs to every Christian, the freedom referred to in 1 Corinthians 6:12 and Galatians 5:1.

The second question ("Am I not an apostle?") shows that Paul could not only claim the liberty that belongs to all Christians, but also the special rights that were attached to the apostolic office. Though the form of the question implies an affirmative response, Paul answers it by asking two additional questions: "Have I not seen Jesus our Lord? Are you not the result of my work in the Lord?" (v. 1b). The former question "points to the foundation of his apostleship, the latter to its visible demonstration" (Bruce).

Findlay observes that the "seeing" here does not describe a "spiritual apprehension" (such as every believer has), "nor the ecstatic visions which [Paul] had sometimes enjoyed in a state of trance (2 Cor. xii. 1ff.), but that actual beholding of the human and glorified Redeemer which befell him on the way to Damascus." The experience was that which qualified Paul to be a witness of the Resurrection (15:8ff.; Gal. 1:15f.) and to be recognized as an apostle (Acts 1:21f.). But since this experience was a matter of Paul's own inner consciousness he points to the very existence of the Corinthian church as an external evidence of his apostleship. "Are you not the result of my work in the Lord?" (v. 1; cf. Rom. 15:15–21). The Damascene vision with its attendant interview was, in its full import, Paul's own private experience; his apostolic power, derived from that experience, "was manifest to the whole world (2 Cor. iii. 1ff., xii. 12), the Corinthian church supplying a conspicuous proof" (Findlay).

Others might doubt Paul's apostleship, but surely the Corinthians should be the last to do so; they were in fact "the seal of [Paul's] apostleship" (v. 2). A "seal" often denoted ownership, but here it connotes authentication.

In verse 3 Paul asserts: "This is my defense to those who sit in judgment on me." The phrase "sit in judgment on me," points back to verses

---

[3]The KJV takes "Am I not an apostle?" to be the opening question of this chapter, but it is better to follow the NIV and others which make "Am I not free?" first.

1b and 2, specifically to the statement that Paul had seen Jesus and that the Corinthians were his work in the Lord. In effect he was saying, "When people question my apostleship, I point them to my vision of the living Christ and to you!"[4]

Having affirmed his freedom as a Christian and the authenticity of his apostleship, Paul now asserts the rights that accompanied his apostleship (vv. 4-6). Three such rights are indicated: (1) the right to financial support by the churches (v. 4), (2) the right to marriage (v. 5), and (3) the right to exemption from manual labor (v. 6). Although recognizing that the underlying idea in each of these is the right of financial support by the churches, we will for convenience' sake discuss them separately.

"Don't we have the right to food and drink?" (v. 4) expects the answer, "Of course we have!" "Right" (KJV, "power"), the key word of this paragraph (six times in 9:1-18) and a link with the preceding chapter (cf. 8:9, where it is translated "freedom"), is the translation of a Greek term (*exousia*) which basically means "*freedom of choice, right* to act, decide, or dispose of one's property as one wishes" (Arndt and Gingrich, *Lexicon*). In an era earlier than the apostolic period, it was a technical term used in legal documents, especially in wills. It came to mean capability, might, power; then authority, persons of authority, and so forth. Here, "right" is the best rendering. "We" is probably best explained as an epistolary plural, though Paul may perhaps use it to include Barnabas (cf. v. 5).

Morris correctly (we think) sees the question of verse 5 ("Don't we have the right to take a believing wife . . . ?") as asserting, not the right of apostles to marry ("Nobody in the apostolic age would have queried this"), but "the right of the apostle, if married, to take his wife with him, the implication being that she, too, would be supported by the church." Barrett thinks there is a double meaning in the question, the first being that "apostles, like other Christians, have a right to be married" and the second being that "apostles, unlike other Christians, have the right to have their wives . . . maintained by the communities in which they are working."

Bruce thinks that special attention is called to Cephas (the Aramaic name of Peter) because his wife may have accompanied him to Corinth. (For a reference to Peter's wife, see Mark 1:30; for the brothers of the Lord, Mark 6:3.) "To lead about a sister, a wife" (ASV) is quite literal, but it is better to render it "to lead about a wife who is a believer." It means to take her along on missionary travels.

The meaning of verse 6 is expressed quite clearly in Phillips' para-

---

[4]Findlay speaks of the Corinthian church as "a shining evidence of Paul's commission" and expresses the opinion that it was "probably the largest church as yet raised in his independent ministry."

phrase: "Are Barnabas and I the only ones not allowed to leave their ordinary work to give time to the ministry?" The question implies that Paul and Barnabas were exceptional in respect to "secular" work, the other apostles customarily refraining from earning their own living while engaged in ministry.

Barrett thinks Paul's mention of Barnabas' name with his own is "probably to be taken as evidence that Barnabas rejoined the Pauline mission" some time after the separation mentioned in Acts 15:39–40. This conclusion, however, should not be pressed. The reference to Barnabas may suggest only that in spite of the sharp contention that had led to their parting company the two men remained on friendly terms.

"To work for a living" is the translation of a term that often, though not always, is used in connection with manual labor (cf. 1 Thess. 4:11; 1 Cor. 4:12).

In verses 1–6 Paul has defended his right to material support from the churches by asserting his equality with the other apostles and with the brothers of the Lord, whose custom it was to receive maintenance from those to whom they ministered. In verses 7–14 he further establishes his right to such support, arguing the question on its own merits. This he does by using illustrations drawn from everyday life (the soldier, the vinedresser, the herdsman, v. 7), by appealing to Scripture (the law of Moses, vv. 8–12), by mentioning the custom of those who performed temple service and/or served at the altar (v. 13), and the teaching of the Lord Himself (v. 14; cf. Matt. 10:10; Luke 10:7).

Only a few matters in these verses require special notice. One is the expression "from a human point of view" (v. 8; Gr., *kata anthropon*, "as a man"). It may simply mean that Paul, in referring to soldiers on duty, vinedressers, and so forth, has used human analogies. However, Barrett expresses a different idea: "You don't suppose do you . . . that I am saying these things with no more than human authority?" This understanding of the phrase has much to commend it.

"Is it about oxen that God is concerned . . . ?" (v. 9b) points up the fact that the directive about muzzling the ox had, in the mind of God, a purpose beyond that of the welfare of oxen: it was intended to teach that the material needs of God's servants be cared for.

In verse 10b the particle translated "that" in KJV is better rendered "for" or "because" (cf. NIV). "Material harvest" in verse 11 (NASB) does not have a bad connotation; it simply refers to "material benefits" (RSV) or "material support" (C. B. Williams).

2. *Paul's willingness to renounce his rights* (9:15–18)

Verses 15–18 show that Paul, though entitled to all the apostolic rights mentioned above, willingly renounced all of them. Verse 15a expresses the essence of it: "But I have not used any of these rights" (cf. v. 12). "I" is emphatic. Others may have used their rights and privileges, but Paul had not. "Have . . . used" is a perfect tense verb, pointing up that this was a settled policy with the apostle. "Any of these rights" refers to the rights enumerated above.

Verse 15b asserts that Paul was not now defending his rights in order to claim them: "And I am not writing this in the hope that you will do such things for me." He suggests in verse 15c that his refusal to avail himself of remuneration for preaching was his ground for boasting, and he would rather die than have anyone rob him of that.[5]

The thought of verses 16–18 is difficult to follow. It seems to be that in the mere act of preaching Paul felt he had nothing of which to boast. He was compelled to do that; "necessity" pressed on him. (MLB: "for preaching the good news I claim no glory, for I am under compulsion to do so.") Therefore if he did not preach, "woe" (some undefined punishment) would come to him. So Paul's real ground for boasting was that he preached the gospel without cost to the people, thus removing all suspicion of selfish motivation.

Conybeare expresses the idea of verse 17 clearly: "For were my service my own free choice, I might claim wages to reward my labour; but since I serve by compulsion, I am a slave entrusted with a stewardship."[6]

In verse 18 Paul declares that preaching without pay was itself his reward, because it meant that he thereby removed a possible hindrance to the gospel.

The previous chapter has insisted that one must, for the sake of his weaker brother, sometimes forego his own rights, limit his freedom, in reference to things morally indifferent. Paul affirms here that he followed such a course for the sake of his work.

3. Other concessions made "for the sake of the gospel" (9:19–23)

Having shown that he had claimed no financial support from the Corinthians lest his motives be misunderstood and his work hindered, the apostle now shows that he made other concessions. Morris sees these verses as bringing out the "extent of Paul's abandonment of his rights in the interests of the gospel." Though "free from all men"—from all human control—he made himself the slave of all in the hope of winning as many

---

[5]The Greek of verse 15c contains a broken construction. It begins with "Better for me to die than ———." This incomplete statement is then followed by an exclamation: "No one will make my boast an empty one!"

[6]Barrett thinks the "reward" includes more than this—not only pay from the churches but a reward from God. Compare the LB, which reads: "If I were volunteering my services of my own free will, then the Lord would give me a special reward."

converts as possible (v. 19)—from among the Jews (v. 20a), those under the law (proselytes? v. 20b), and those not under the law (pagans, v. 21).

This same tender concern had been manifest in Paul's dealings with "the weak" (overscrupulous believers, v. 22a). Among them he behaved as though he shared their scruples. The matter is summarized in verse 22b: "I have become all things to all men so that by all possible means I might save some."

Verse 23 states Paul's motive: All things are done "for the sake of the gospel, that I may share in its blessings." "For the sake of the gospel" reveals that the apostle's whole course of action was regulated by the gospel. To "share in its blessings" means to be a partaker (along with others) of its benefits. "It is necessary to live for the gospel, in order to be a partaker of the gospel" (Hodge).

C. Liberty Limited by Solicitude for One's Own Well-Being (9:24–10:22)

Thus far, in his treatment of the question of eating meat sacrificed to idols, Paul has employed two lines of reasoning. One has to do with *concern for the well-being of weaker believers*. For the "strong" to exercise their liberty (right) by indulging in questionable practices may cause spiritual injury to the "weak" (the overscrupulous). Consideration of this should lead the strong to regulate their liberty by love (8:1–13). The other line of reasoning has to do with *concern for the unimpeded progress of the gospel*. Using his own experience as an example, Paul shows that this will lead one to forego his own rights and exercise his freedom with caution (9:1–23).

The unit we are now approaching (9:24–10:22) sounds a solemn warning to the "strong": it is perilous for their own souls if they give in to self-indulgence and complacency. A good text for the entire unit might be: "If you think you are standing firm, be careful that you don't fall!" (10:12).

The argument is presented on three levels. First, Paul speaks of his own experience, reminding the Corinthians that he practiced an austere and continuing self-discipline for fear that after having preached to others he himself should be disqualified and forfeit the wreath of victory (9:24–27). Next, the apostle cites the experience of Israel, who upon coming out of Egypt presumed on the favor of God and suffered His displeasure (10:1–13). Finally, appealing to the intelligence of the Corinthians, he uses their own everyday experience to argue the impossibility of sharing both the table of the Lord and the table of demons (10:14–22).

1. *The experience of Paul* (9:24–27)

In chapter 8 Paul contended that Christians should look after the interests of their weaker brothers and sisters. Here, using the example of his own life, he pressed on his readers the need to look after their own spiritual interests. Since the appeal was addressed to gentile converts, he used imagery drawn from the public games that were familiar to them ("Do you not know . . . ?" v. 24a). The reference could be to the Olympic games but it is more likely to the Isthmian games, held every two years in the vicinity of Corinth. The games consisted of five contests: leaping, discus-throwing, running, boxing, and wrestling. Paul's discussion alludes to two of these, running (v. 24) and boxing (vv. 26b, 27a).

"Do you not know . . . ?" (v. 24) implies an affirmative answer. Paul assumed that his readers were familiar with the rules and customs pertaining to the games. He mentioned first that though *all* the participants in the race ran, only *one* received the prize (v. 24a). The Corinthians were urged to run the race of the Christian life like that one, persevering to the end and with full resolve to win (v. 24b). "In the Christian race there are many victors; but the point of the exhortation is, that all should run as the one victor ran in the Grecian games" (Hodge). "The Christian must not only start but continue in the right way; it is implied that he must put forth all his strength" (Barrett).

Paul's next point is that all participants in the contests practice "self-control in all things" (v. 25a, NASB). The reference is to the period of training that preceded the games. "Goes into strict training" (NIV) is a free rendering of a word the root meaning of which is "to exercise mastery over oneself." "In all things" (RSV, ASV) probably means in every way. (Conybeare: "and every man who strives in the matches trains himself by all manner of self-restraint.") For the ten-month period preceding the games all the participants were required, under oath, to follow a prescribed diet, abstain from various bodily indulgences, and go through vigorous training. For thirty days just prior to the games all contestants were required to attend exercises in the gymnasium.

Finally, Paul contrasted the perishable wreath of pine leaves, which was the athlete's reward, with the imperishable crown the Christian receives at the end of his race (v. 25b). Morris's words are apropos:

> The strenuous self-denial of the athlete in training for his fleeting reward is a rebuke to all half-hearted, flabby Christian service. Notice that the athlete denies himself many lawful pleasures. The Christian must avoid not only definite sin, but anything that hinders his complete effectiveness.

Edwards observes that there are two lessons taught in verse 25: "the difficulty of winning and the unspeakable worth of the prize."

In verse 26 the imagery is still that of the games, although the stress is not on discipline in training but the controlled effort in the contest itself. Paul does not run like a runner who does not know where the finish line is. Nor does he live without purpose, like a boxer punching the air. (The expression suggests either shadow boxing or missing one's opponent.)

Verse 27 is the positive statement of what is put negatively in verse 26. "I beat my body and make it my slave." "He not only hits, but he bruises, and his antagonist is his own body" (Edwards). The Greek for "beat," a strong expression for treating roughly, literally means "to strike under the eye," "to give a black eye to." ("Keep under," KJV, is the translation of a different but similar-sounding word.) The "body" is so treated, not because it is an enemy in itself evil, but because it is both the weapon with which sin fights us, and "the sphere within which the spiritual powers of evil come within our reach to be bruised and destroyed" (Edwards). Barrett comments that

> Paul recognizes the need to beat his body out of its all too ready obedience to sin, in order that it may be brought into the service of God. The body is not evil, but it must be made to serve the right master, not the wrong one.

Findlay cautions against the misuse of this text, citing "the Middle-Age Flagellants and similar self-torturers" who justified their practices by it. We should remember that the language, graphic and sobering and powerful, is not to be interpreted literally. Indeed, the passage really describes the severity with which one must treat not his body, but his bodily appetites.

Paul's purpose in thus disciplining himself is stated in verse 27b: "so that, after I have preached to others [served as herald summoning others into the arena] I myself will not be disqualified" (v. 27b). The allusion is to the examination of the participants at the close of the contest. If it was then revealed that the winner did not contend according to the rules of the game, he forfeited his crown. "After I have preached" translates a Greek word that means "to herald." The noun built on the same root was used of the "herald" at the games, whose responsibility it was to summon the competitors and explain the rules of the contest.

The word for "disqualified" essentially denotes something/someone that has "not stood the test." Hodge understands the word as relating to salvation.

> The reckless and listless Corinthians thought they could safely indulge themselves to the very verge of sin, while this devoted apostle considered himself as engaged in a life-struggle for his salvation. This same apostle, however, who evidently acted on the principle that the righteous scarcely are saved, and that the kingdom of heaven suffereth violence, at other times breaks out in the most joyful assurance of salvation, and says that he was persuaded that nothing in heaven, earth or hell could ever separate him from the love of God. Rom. 8:38,39. The one state of mind is the necessary

condition of the other. It is only those who are conscious of this constant and deadly struggle with sin, to whom this assurance is given. In the very same breath Paul says, 'O wretched man that I am;' and, 'Thanks be to God who giveth us the victory,' Rom. 7:24–25. It is the indolent and self-indulgent Christian who is always in doubt.

Morris writes: "Paul's fear was not that he might lose his salvation, but that he might lose his crown through failing to satisfy his Lord (cf. iii. 15)." Others think the reference might be to loss of place of service.

2. The tragic example of Israel (10:1–13)

The reader should not let the connection of this paragraph with 9:24–27 be obscured by the chapter division. The discipline and determination that characterized Paul's life found no place in the lives of many of the Israelites who followed Moses out of Egypt. In spite of their special privileges and advantages, they gave in to idolatry and lust, and in so doing they presumed on the favor of God and suffered disaster.

Paul used Israel's experience to warn the Corinthians not to make the same mistake. They were not to see how far they could go before God would punish them. They were not to test the forbearance and mercy of God. They were to follow those ways they knew to be right. The passage should be seen as a solemn warning against complacency and over-confidence.

The privileges of "our forefathers" are recounted in verses 1–4. Notice the repetition of the word "all." *All* were "under [the guidance of] the cloud." The allusion is to the shekinah, the visible manifestation of the presence of God among the Israelites. The idea is that they all had experienced the divine presence and guidance. *All* "passed through the sea" (experienced miraculous deliverance).

Verse 2a summarizes the two experiences affirmed in verse 1. *All* were "baptized into [in connection with, in reference to] Moses in the cloud and in the sea." The meaning seems to be that by following the guidance of the cloud and by experiencing deliverance from the sea they all acknowledged Moses to be their divinely appointed leader and pledged themselves to follow him. (Goodspeed: "all, as it were, accepted baptism as followers of Moses.") Paul probably used the figure of "baptism" because he was thinking of Moses as a type of Christ. By participating in the great events of the Exodus the Israelites acknowledged the divinely purposed role of Moses; in Christian baptism believers acknowledge Christ as their deliverer and leader.

All "ate the same spiritual [supernatural, RSV] food" and *all* drank "the same spiritual drink" (vv. 3, 4a). The reference is to the manna supplied

from heaven and the water the people drank from "the spiritual rock that
accompanied them." These latter words may *allude* to a Jewish legend of
a rock following Israel throughout their wanderings in the wilderness.
Paul, however, makes his meaning quite clear: the "spiritual rock" was
Christ (v. 4). Hodge explains that Christ is the "rock in the same sense
that he is the vine." "He was the source of all the support which the
Israelites enjoyed during their journey in the wilderness."

Verse 5 teaches that it is not enough to be recipients of divine favors; it
is not enough to make a good beginning. The promised reward can be
obtained only by constant self-denial and vigilance. All the Israelites who
left Egypt were favored alike and therefore had the same ground for
hope, but how few of them entered the Promised Land! With "most of
them God was not pleased." Morris calls this "a masterly understatement," since only two men out of the hosts of Israel actually entered
Canaan. The rest were "scattered over the desert." The language
pictures the wilderness as strewn with the corpses of disobedient
Israelites.

Verse 6a affirms that Israel's experience, as recorded in the Scriptures,
stands as a warning to all of us. "These things occurred as examples." The
Greek behind the word "examples" literally means types. "The Israelites
and the facts of their history were our types," explains Hodge, "because
we shall be conformed to them if we do not exercise caution. Our doom
will correspond to theirs."

The idea of Israel's example as warning is expanded in verses 6b–10.
The history of Israel is a warning to us not to set "our hearts on evil
things" (v. 6b), not to be idolaters (v. 7), not to commit sexual immorality
(v. 8),[7] not to test the Lord (v. 9), and not to murmur (grumble, complain)
(v. 10).

The "destroying angel" (Phillips: "Angel of Death") of verse 10 was an
angel sent by God to use pestilence as an instrument of destruction. The
reference is to Numbers, perhaps chapter 11, perhaps chapter 14, or
perhaps chapter 16.

Verse 11 is a summing up of the foregoing verses. All these things
happened in such a way as to leave us an example (repeating the thought
of v. 6a), and they were recorded to serve as a caution to us, "on whom
the ends of the ages have come" (literal translation). This is a difficult
phrase but its essential meaning seems clear enough: Christians are people living in the closing age of the world. The successive periods of human
history have run their course, and with the arrival of the Christian era the

---

[7]Observe the close connection of idolatry (v. 7) and sexual immorality (v. 8) and bear in
mind that this entire unit of 1 Corinthians is dealing with a matter connected with idol
worship.

climax of the ages has been reached. Bruce suggests that "ends" has simply been attracted to the plural number of the word "ages." The meaning is "the end," the culmination of the ages. There is probably the added idea, suggested by the context, of fulfillment. This is the interpretation reflected in the NIV: "on whom the fulfillment of the ages has come."

Verses 12 and 13 round out this unit by sounding a solemn warning against overconfidence (v. 12) and by giving a message of encouragement and cheer (v. 13). The *warning* was especially needed by the "strong" (the libertarians), for all that Paul has said in this section suggests that they were especially prone to be overconfident.

"If you think you are standing firm" means "let him who thinks he is secure." The reference may be to the security of salvation or to security against the power of temptation.

> False security of salvation commonly rests on the ground of our belonging to a privileged body (the church), or to a privileged class (the elect). Both are equally fallacious. Neither the members of the church nor the elect can be saved unless they persevere in holiness; and they cannot persevere in holiness without continual watchfulness and effort. False security as to our power to resist temptation rests on an overweening self-confidence in our own strength. None are so liable to fall as they who, thinking themselves strong, heedlessly run into temptation. This probably is the kind of false security against which the apostle warns the Corinthians, as he exhorts them immediately after to avoid temptation (Hodge).

The "fall" envisioned is a moral fall involving personal ruin. The whole statement suggests that there is constant danger of falling. "No degree of progress we may have already made, no amount of privileges which we may have enjoyed, can justify the want of caution" (Hodge).

The *encouragement* alludes to the fact that the hardships experienced by Israel in the wilderness were a part of God's plan to test His people, for the purpose of bringing out their true character (cf. Deut. 8:2). The suggestion is that the temptations to which the Corinthian Christians were being subjected might serve the same purpose for them. "Temptation" is the translation of a word that can mean enticement to evil (which is the meaning of the English word today), or it can mean testing in general and include trials of every kind. God does not entice us to do evil but He does test His people. Satan entices—always with evil intent; God tests—but always with good intent (cf. James 1:13–18). The words "temptation" and "tempted" should probably be understood in the broad sense of trial or test, of whatever kind. The specific "temptation" of the Corinthians was the allurement of idolatry and the persecution/ostracization that its abandonment brought.

To keep the Corinthians from despair, they were reminded of two things: (1) There was nothing exceptional about their experience; nothing had befallen them that is not the common lot of mankind. The depressing catalog of Israel's experiences (vv. 1–10) underlines this fact. It shows that the trials of the Corinthians were not unprecedented. (2) God is faithful (TCNT: "God will not fail you")[8]: He could be trusted not to permit[9] them to be tempted/tested beyond their ability to resist and overcome. God limits trials and with them provides a way out, making it possible for the persons tested to hold out under them. Findlay writes: "Shut into a *cul de sac*, a man despairs; but let him see a door open for his exit, and he will struggle on with his load." Morris observes that the Greek word for "way to escape" (KJV) "may denote a mountain defile. The imagery is that of an army trapped in the mountains, which escapes from an impossible situation through a pass."

3. *The perilous situation of the Corinthians* (10:14–22)

The topic of discussion that began at 8:1 and which continues through 11:1 arose out of the question whether Christians should eat the sacrifices offered to idols. Though contending that there was nothing unlawful about eating such food, Paul has throughout urged abstinence—out of consideration for the "weak conscience" of those who were overly scrupulous (ch. 8), out of concern for the larger interests of the gospel (9:1–23), and out of concern about the consequences of self-indulgence (9:24–10:13). In this passage, continuing the emphasis of the preceding paragraph, he warns his readers against participation in sacrificial feasts within the precincts of the pagan temple (10:14–22).

The object of this discussion is to show that attendance at a feast in a pagan temple is an act of idolatry. The structure is as follows: (1) It begins with an urgent command to "flee from idolatry" (v. 14). Verse 13 has spoken of a "way out" of temptations. Verse 14 suggests that sometimes *flight* is the only way out. Believers must not deliberately enter tempta-

---

[8]Hodge writes that "the security of believers is referred neither to the strength of the principle of grace infused into them by regeneration, nor to their own firmness, but to the fidelity of God. He has promised that those given to the Son as his inheritance, should never perish. They are kept, therefore, by the power of God, through faith, unto salvation, 1 Peter 1, 4. This promise of security, however, is a promise of security from sin, and therefore those who fall into wilful and habitual sin are not the subjects of the promise. Should they fall, it is after a severe struggle, and they are soon renewed again unto repentance. The absolute security of believers, and the necessity of constant watchfulness, are perfectly consistent. Those whom God has promised to save, he has promised to render watchful."

[9]Findlay comments that "Paul ascribes to God not the origination, but the *control* of temptation."

tions and then expect deliverance. "They must not try how near they can go, but how far they can fly" (Robertson and Plummer).

The Greek verb for "flee" means "to seek safety in flight." In a moral sense, as here, it means to "avoid," "shun," "run away from." The tense is present, indicating habitual action. It might therefore be rendered, "Keep on running away from idolatry." The affectionate address ("my dear friends"; lit., "my beloved"), not common in Paul's letters, brings out something of the depth of his emotions and assures his readers that he had their welfare at heart. In effect, it turns the command into an entreaty.

(2) The appeal to avoid idolatry is enforced by a reference to the implications of participation in the Lord's Supper (vv. 15–17). The passage begins with an invitation to the readers to sit in judgment on the validity of the instructions that follow: "Look now and see for yourselves whether what I am about to say is true" (LB). By addressing them as "sensible men" (NIV) Paul was recognizing their ability to see the soundness of his argument. "I appeal to your intelligence" (MLB). Hodge adds that "should they differ from the apostle, that would not alter the case. . . . But he takes this way of convincing them."

In verses 16 and 17 it is explained that attendance at the table of the Lord is an act of communion (participation, fellowship) with Him. The drinking of the wine and the eating of the bread in some way constitute fellowship with the blood and body of Christ. Fisher observes that this passage should not be used to support modern ecclesiastical practice with regard to the Supper, adding that Paul's main statement on the meaning of the Lord's Supper is in 1 Corinthians 11. The present passage brings in the Supper only "by way of comparison, and the comparison has perhaps influenced the language."

(3) The same principle holds true of the sacrifices offered by Jews. Whoever partook of those sacrifices was engaging in an act of worship (v. 18). (4) The obvious conclusion is that to participate in a feast at a pagan temple is to share in the worship of the idol (vv. 19,20). One cannot be a worshiper of Christ and at the same time be a worshiper of demons. Sharing at the table of the Lord is a renunciation of demons; sharing at the table of demons is a renunciation of Christ (v. 21) and will provoke His jealousy (v. 22).

Only a few matters call for specific comment. The "cup of thanksgiving" (v. 16; "cup of blessing," ASV, RSV), which refers to the cup of the Lord's Supper, is so called because a thanksgiving was pronounced over it. The phrase does not mean "the cup that brings blessing." In describing the cup as "a participation in the blood of Christ" and the bread as "a participation in the body of Christ" (v. 16) Paul meant that the participants at the Lord's Supper shared in the benefits of His blood shed for us and of His body given for us.[10] Bruce concludes that "neither the blood nor the body has a material sense here; the point is that in the Eucharist the communicants partake jointly of the life of Christ."

"One loaf" is mentioned because in New Testament times a single loaf was used in celebrating the Supper. The thought is that just as the many fragments of broken bread make up one loaf, so believers, though many, make up one body. The one loaf thus symbolizes the unity of the people of God.

"The people of Israel" (lit., "Israel after the flesh"; v. 18) is the nation Israel as distinguished from Christians, the Israel of God (Gal. 3:29; 6:16; Phil. 3:3), Israel after the Spirit.

Verses 19 and 20 should be read alongside 8:4. When both verses are rightly interpreted there is no inconsistency. The question of verse 19 implies the answer "No." In a sense there was no reality in either the idol or the thing sacrificed to it. The thing sacrificed was professedly an offering to a god, and the idol was supposed to represent a god.

> Both were shams. The [thing sacrificed] was just a piece of flesh and nothing more, and its being sacrificed to a being that had no existence did not alter that quality; the meat was neither the better nor the worse for that. The [idol] was just so much metal, or wood, or stone, and its being supposed to represent a being that had no existence did not alter its value; it was neither more nor less useful than before. As a sacrifice to a god, and as the image of a god, the [thing sacrificed] and the [idol] had no reality, for there was no such being as Aphrodite or Serapis. Nevertheless, there was something behind both, although not what was believed to be there (Robertson and Plummer).[11]

"Devils" (KJV) in verse 20 should be read "demons." There is only one devil (Gr., *diabolos*), but there are many demons (Gr., *daimonia*), who are to be understood as evil spirits or fallen angels.

"The sacrifices . . . are offered . . . not to God" (v. 20) perhaps is better read "they sacrifice . . . to a no-god." Compare Deuteronomy 32:21,

---

[10]Hodge appropriately explains that "this, of course, is true only of believers. Paul is writing to believers, and assumes the presence of faith in the receiver."

[11]Hodge's comments are worth quoting: "The heathen certainly did not intend to worship evil spirits. Nevertheless they did it. Men of the world do not intend to serve Satan, when they break the laws of God in the pursuit of their objects of desire. Still in so doing they are really obeying the will of the great adversary, yielding to his impulses, and fulfilling his designs. He is therefore said to be the god of this world. To him all sin is an offering and an homage. We are shut up to the necessity of worshipping God or Satan for all refusing or neglecting to worship the true God, or giving to any other the worship which is due to him alone, is the worshipping of Satan and his angels. It is true therefore, in the highest sense, that what the heathen offer they offer to devils.

which seems to confirm this view: "They made me jealous by what is no god and angered me with their worthless idols. I will make them envious by those who are not a people" (NIV). Robertson and Plummer remark that the rendering "not to God" introduces a superfluous thought: "there was no need to declare that sacrifices to idols are not offered to God. But 'to a no-god' has point."

The essential teaching of verse 21 is that the Lord's Supper is a feeding at the Lord's table (i.e., the table presided over by Him) and an occasion of fellowship with Him. Similarly, participation in a pagan feast in the idol temple is to eat at the table of demons and to have fellowship with them. This makes it a moral impossibility—not just an incongruity or an inconsistency—for Christians to participate at both "tables."

The better Greek manuscripts have the word for "or" at the beginning of verse 22. (It is not translated in the NIV and is omitted in the text underlying the KJV.) The meaning may be paraphrased: "I have assumed that you Corinthians do not understand the significance of going to a feast at the idol temple, and the foregoing explanation is given accordingly. But perhaps you do understand. That puts the whole matter in a different light, for then you must be deliberately provoking the Lord to jealousy— an extremely foolish course of action unless you are stronger than He!"

Hodge comments that "jealousy is the feeling which arises from wounded love, and is the fiercest of all human passions. It is therefore employed as an illustration of the hatred of God towards idolatry."

D. The Concluding Summary, Offering Practical Suggestions for the Guidance of the Corinthians (10:23–11:1)[12]

Paul now brings his long discussion of the question of sacrificial food to a close;[13] in doing so he recapitulates the salient points of his argument and states the great comprehensive principles by which all questions of conscience are to be resolved.

---

[12]Barrett gives to this passage the heading "Nature, Extent, and Limitations of Christian Freedom." Similarly, Findlay titles it "Liberty and Its Limits." Edwards calls it "A Practical Summary," explaining that the section is "a reiteration in a more practical form of [Paul's] doctrine of liberty and love." Hodge sees it as a setting forth of the circumstances under which Christians could eat sacrificial meat.

[13]It is well to remind ourselves again that throughout this section (8:1–11:1) the specific problem dealt with is whether to eat sacrificial meat, but the larger problem is Christian liberty. Stonehouse, in the preface to Grosheide's commentary on this epistle, has words penetrating and clear: "At times Paul was concerned with 'the weak,' whose attitude toward things sacrificed to idols betrayed a failure to grasp the principles of Christian liberty. . . . But the main thrust of the Epistle is directed . . . against those whose life principles were quite the opposite: the spiritually proud and 'puffed up,' who boasted of their 'knowledge' and of their 'rights.' Their temper was expressed by the rule, 'All things are lawful unto me,' and this declaration of freedom was made the ultimate and only principle of conduct."

The passage may be seen as setting forth three fundamental guidelines for Christian conduct in matters of conscience: (1) the good of other believers (vv. 23–30), (2) the glory of God (v. 31), and (3) the example of Christ (10:32–11:1).

1. *The principle of concern for others* (10:23–30)

This principle is stated (vv. 23–24) and then applied (vv. 25–30).

The statement (vv. 23–24). Christian liberty is reaffirmed ("Everything is permissible," v. 23),[14] but Paul quickly qualifies it by three other considerations: "not everything is beneficial" (v. 23b), "not everything is constructive" (v. 23d), and "Nobody should seek his own good, but the good of others" (v. 24). These three statements really say much the same thing, namely, *liberty should be limited by consideration for the well-being of others.*

We may be free to pursue a given course of action, but we must ask ourselves if it is "beneficial" (v. 23a; RSV, "helpful"; TCNT, "profitable") to do so. It is open to question whether Paul was thinking of the effect of one's actions on one's own life or on others. Moffatt has "good for us"; Beck, "good for others." Again, all things are lawful (permissible), but will the doing of them be "constructive" (v. 23d)? As with "beneficial," it is difficult to know whether the reference is to one's own life or to others. Conybeare has "build up the church"; TCNT, "build up character." Perhaps we should not try to be precise in our interpretation, letting both of these qualifying expressions include the interests of self and of others. Our own feeling is that the primary reference in each is the welfare of other people.

Verse 24 enforces these thoughts by affirming that every Christian, in the use of his liberty, is to have regard for the welfare[15] of others. That is to say, we should be guided not exclusively by regard for our own interests, but also by consideration for the good of others. A Christian has the abstract right to do whatever is not in itself wrong, but consideration for the good of others places practical limits on this right (liberty).

The application (vv. 25–30). Having affirmed this all-embracing principle of concern for the good of others Paul now deals with concrete cases (vv. 25–30). First, there is the question of eating meat purchased at the

---

[14]"Everything is permissible" appears to have been a slogan used by the libertarians in defense of eating sacrificial meat and indulging in other questionable things (cf. discussion of 6:12 and observe the use of quotation marks in NEB, NIV, and other modern versions). Fisher cautions that "Everything" must be taken in a restricted sense. "It means all food, not all actions."

[15]KJV has "wealth," which in 1611 meant "welfare," "good," "benefit."

market (vv. 25–26). This may be done without raising any questions or indulging any scruples about the source of the meat. That which is purchased at the market is to be thought of not as a sacrifice to an idol but as food provided by a loving God for the use of mankind. "The earth is the LORD's, and everything in it"; therefore all food that it produces is to be gratefully received as a gift of God.

Second, there is the question of eating sacrificial meat when one is a guest in a private home (vv. 27–30). Even then the Christian is free to eat what is placed before him unless someone calls attention to the food's association with idols.[16] In that case the Christian should not eat it, for the sake of the person who has brought up the matter, and for conscience' sake. The reference in the latter words is not to the conscience of the eater (who is obviously one of the "strong" and has no scruples about the matter) but of someone else, either the informant (which is probable) or some other person at the meal. The statement is somewhat awkward, but the thought is that the person (whoever he is) would be shocked, and the shock would be a shock to conscience.

> A present-day analogy may be imagined if someone with strong principles on total abstention from alcohol were the guest of friends who did not share these principles. He would be well advised not to enquire too carefully about the ingredients of some specially palatable sauce or trifle, but if someone said to him pointedly, 'There is alcohol in this, you know', he might feel that he was being put on the spot and could reasonably ask to be excused from having any of it (Bruce).

Verses 29b and 30 contain two rhetorical questions that justify[17] the "strong" Christian's deference to the conscience of another. In both questions Paul "graphically puts himself in the place of the Christian guest

---

[16]This is a clear indication that the situation envisioned takes place in a private home. At an idol feast there would be no need for anyone to say, "This has been offered in sacrifice." The identity of the speaker is less certain. It is obviously a fellow guest, not the host (whose conscience would not be bothered). Also, it appears that the speaker must be a Christian (a "weak" brother who is overly scrupulous). Finally, the use of *hierothyton* (a pagan term for "sacred sacrifice") rather than *eidolothyton* (the customary Jewish term for "idol sacrifice") strongly suggests the speaker was a gentile believer.

[17]Some understand the words to be the *objection* of a strong Christian to having his liberty limited by the conscience of others. Paul, anticipating the objection, stated it himself: "But, you may object, why should my freedom be decided upon another's scruples of conscience?" (Montgomery). C. B. Williams expresses the same understanding: "Why then should my personal freedom be limited by another's conscience?" If this is the correct construction to be placed on the words, it is strange that Paul does not answer the objection. Moreover, if the question was intended as an objection it would naturally have been introduced by "but," not "for."

who has been placed in a difficulty by the officiousness of his scrupulous informant" (Robertson and Plummer). The sense of the first question is expressed by Findlay in paraphrase: "What good end will be served by my eating under these circumstances, and exposing my freedom to the censure of an unsympathetic conscience?" It is implied that nothing is to be gained by insisting on one's liberty under these circumstances. Indeed, verse 30, by means of a second question, suggests that the result will be slander from those who lack the perspective and knowledge of the "strong." Beck brings out the sense of this question: "why should I let myself be denounced for eating what I thank God for?"

2. *The principle of God's glory* (10:31)

The Greek word for "glory" means "brightness," "splendor," "radiance," then "fame," "renown," "honor." Here the idea is honor. This is the most comprehensive principle of all, in a sense embracing all others. Eating or drinking or anything else must be subordinated to it. Hodge expresses the meaning well: "Let self be forgotten. Let your eye be fixed on God. Let the promotion of his glory be your object in all you do. Strive in everything to act in such a way that men may praise that God whom you profess to serve."

3. *The example of Christ* (10:32–11:1)

In these verses Paul charges his readers to give no occasion of stumbling to anybody[18] (v. 32), points to his own practice (v. 33),[19] and urges the Corinthians to pattern their lives after his, even as he patterns his life after that of Christ (11:1). Though most of this statement has to do with Paul and his example for the Corinthians, the climax is reached when he affirms that he is an imitator of Christ. The language suggests that Paul is worthy of imitation only to the extent that he himself is an imitator of his Lord. It seems therefore that the ultimate purpose of the passage is to hold up for emulation the example of Jesus Christ. Barrett explains that "there is no hierarchy of mediated imitation here. But Paul is wise enough to know that his own imitation of Christ was, if imperfect, a good deal more accessible than the historic life of Jesus."

At the beginning of this chapter attention was called to three aspects of the problem of sacrificial foods. Looking back over Paul's treatment of the

---

[18]Jews and Greeks embrace all those who are unbelievers; the church of God, made up of all Christians, is a "third race."

[19]To "please," which means to accommodate oneself to, is explained by the words that follow: "not seeking my own good, but the good of many."

matter, we may now summarize his conclusions. First, eating at temple feasts has been shown to be idolatry and is therefore forbidden (10:14–22). Second, eating meat bought at the market, which may or may not have a connection with idols, is unreservedly permitted (10:25–26). Third, whether to eat food or not to eat it at nonceremonial occasions in a private home is to be determined in light of circumstances. If no one calls attention to its connection with idols, it is to be eaten (10:27). If, however, attention is called to the association of the food with idols, out of deference to the scruples of those present, the eating of the food is prohibited—not because the act is in itself wrong, but because it might offend a weaker brother (10:28–30).

For Further Study

1. Read Galatians 5:1–15 and Romans 14:1–15:13. In the former passage observe what is taught about Christian liberty. Notice that liberty may be denied by a spirit of legalism; it may be perverted by license. In the Romans passage notice the reference to the "strong" and the "weak." Compare the teachings of the passage with similar references in chapters 8–10 of 1 Corinthians.

2. Study Mark 7:1–23. Does the teaching of these verses have any bearing on the discussion of eating meat offered to idols?

3. Read an article in an encyclopedia on the Greek games (Isthmian and/or Olympic).

4. Read about perseverance and/or the security of the believer in a Bible dictionary (such as Zondervan's) or a work on theology. You may wish to check your church library for the latter.

Chapter 6

The Veiling of Women in Public Worship
(1 Corinthians 11:2–16)

In previous sections of 1 Corinthians Paul has dealt with matters of personal morality and behavior. He now gives directions concerning the worship of the church as a body. He is concerned that the women of Corinth not express their new freedom in Christ by flouting cherished customs that reflect God's order (11:2–16).

Paul's words of praise in 11:2 introduce one of his most difficult passages from the standpoint of modern application. The Corinthians were likely aware of Paul's teaching that in Christ there is neither male nor female (Gal. 3:28). Some of the Corinthian women may have inquired whether or not the conventional social custom of a veil for the women should be maintained in the light of their new spiritual freedom.[1] In giving his answer Paul is not speaking of how women should dress in public but how they should dress in the practice of group worship. The covering for the head in this passage should be "understood as a head-covering concealing the hair and upper part of the body, not as a covering for the face" (Barrett).

In the New Testament world there was a considerable diversity about the wearing of these veils in different ethnic groups. Morris notes that Jewish men, then as they do now, prayed with their heads covered.[2] Greek men and women prayed with heads uncovered (Morris), and Roman men appear to have prayed with heads covered (Gundry).

Faced with a variety of customs, Paul felt it necessary to define a strictly Christian practice. He appeals to the relative status of men and women in the created order, suggesting that woman's creation from man implies her submission to him. Even though man and woman are one in

---

[1]Even though the specific problem of the passage concerns the wearing of the veil, the larger problem deals with the relationship of the man and the woman.

[2]Craig believes that Jewish men in the first century did not cover their heads for prayer but that the custom arose in the fourth century.

Christ and thus spiritually equal, the distinction given in creation is not annulled.

Paul suggests that women should wear a veil as a symbol of subordination to the husband and as a symbol of modesty. In the case of an unmarried woman the wearing of the veil would suggest a subordination to the father or to a guardian. The wearing of this veil would distinguish a Christian woman from some other woman whose head had been shaven because of grief (Deut. 21:12), some form of moral disgrace, or some type of shameless activity.

Paul defends his directive with numerous reasons. After beginning with a word of praise in 11:2, he affirms the principle of subordination of the woman to the man (v. 3). Such a subordination should not be seen as reflecting inferiority or less worth but different functions or roles. In verses 4–6 Paul deduces two conclusions from the principles of verse 3. The man is not to veil or cover his head because this would obscure God's image and glory. The woman should veil her head, for to refuse this would dishonor her husband, her head. Paul defends these inferences in verses 7–10 by saying that these differences in sexual roles are rooted in creation itself. In verses 11 and 12 he warns against concluding from his observations that woman is inferior to man. Indeed, both man and woman owe their existence to the other, and together they form a unity that shows their mutual dependence. Paul appeals to the Corinthians' sense of propriety and to the teaching of nature in verses 13–15. What he has suggested is seen as a custom in all the churches (v. 16).

The multiplication of reasons for enforcing his injunction may indicate that Paul felt the difficulty of the custom he was urging. He almost seems to be feeling his way through the matter as he writes.

A. A Statement of Praise (11:2)

Paul begins his instruction to the Corinthians with tact and thoughtfulness. He was pleased that they remembered him and held fast to the traditions he had taught. Paul makes reference to traditions in 11:23; 15:1,3; Romans 6:17 and in 2 Thessalonians 2:15; 3:6. These traditions were handed on orally from teacher or evangelist and concerned the basic facts of the gospel, plus some training in conduct.

B. The Principle of Subordination (11:3)

Barrett feels that "head" here speaks of the man, or the husband, as the origin of the being of woman. More likely the term "indicates a relationship of superior authority, but it does not define that authority with precision" (Morris). The potentially absolute nature of this relationship is modified by the husband's submission to Christ (Eph. 5:23). The principle of subordination is operative within the Godhead in that the Father is the head of Christ. Christ is as truly God as is the Father. He is equal in essence, but He is subordinate in function and role.

Paul intends his readers to understand the subordinate role of the woman as seen in creation, but he does not see this as suggesting inferiority. Nor does the subordinate nature of the woman suggest that she is less important than the man. Paul's discussion relates to her position in an organization structure. Paul, however, "is not arguing for anything other than a partnership . . . , though a partnership in which the man is the head of his household" (Morris).

C. Conclusions Based on Woman's Subordination (11:4–6)

Paul first concludes (v. 4) that a man is not to cover his head. The use of a covering or veil on the head was the sign of being under authority to another human being. Since the man was not subject to any other creature, he dishonored his head by covering it while praying. In God's created order those present in worship with a man would either be his equals or his inferiors, and thus no covering would be necessary. The first appearance of "head" in verse 4 is a reference to the physical head of the man. Commentators differ as to whether the second reference speaks of the man's physical head or his spiritual head, Jesus Christ. The application is little different with either meaning, but it seems more likely that Paul is saying that covering the head of a man in prayer dishonors his true head, Jesus Christ, the only one to whom the man owes submission.

For the woman there is a different conclusion (vv. 5–6). She is to wear a covering in worship. To refuse to cover her physical head is to dishonor her husband, who is her head. Commentators differ as to whether the second use of "head" in verse 5 speaks of the physical head of the woman or of the husband. In light of the symbolic usage of head in verse 4 it seems likely that head in verse 5 is a reference to the husband. Paul's statement in verse 5 about the woman who "prays or prophesies" suggests that there was liberty in the church for women to pray or prophesy, but they were not to abuse this privilege, as he points out in 14:34 and 35 (Bruce). Hillyer notes that "for a woman in Corinth to be unveiled in public was as shocking in its social significance as being *shorn*, the contemporary punishment for a prostitute." The TCNT captures the spirit of this prohibition when it says: "To cut her hair short, or shave it off, marks her as one of the shameless women."

In these verses Paul commands the veiling of the woman under the assumption that wearing the veil is a symbol of respectability. God has made a distinction between the man and the woman, and the wearing of the veil is an effort to manifest that distinction.

D. Support for the Principle of Subordination (11:7–10)

To support the principle, Paul now appeals to the biblical account of creation (vv. 7–10). Paul's statements are thus not rooted merely in social custom or convention but are reflected in creation itself. There is a divine order of the sexes.

To buttress his views, Paul refers in verse 7 to Genesis 1:26 and 27, where man is said to have been created in the image of God. The reference to man in Genesis speaks of both the male and the female, but Paul draws conclusions only for the male and then moves in his thinking to Genesis 2:18–23, which emphasizes that the woman was created from the man. To say that man is created in the image of God describes him as a rational and morally responsible person. The term "glory" refers to that which is secondary in contrast to the original (Craig). Thus, the male is the secondary copy of God, and the woman is the secondary copy of the man. The man must not wear a covering, for he is by original constitution the image and glory of God. To veil man's head would obscure God's image and detract from His glory.

In verses 8 and 9 Paul states that neither in her origin nor in the purpose for her creation can woman claim priority over man. In her origin as narrated in Genesis 2:21 woman was made out of a rib drawn from Adam's side. As to her purpose she was a helper to man (Gen. 2:18). Williams states in verse 9, "Man was not created for woman's sake, but woman was for man's sake."

What Paul is describing in verses 8 and 9 is the role of woman as established at creation. According to Galatians 3:28 this old order has been transcended in Christ by the order of the new creation. However, Paul still insists that those in Christ should show respect for the old order by their dress and their behavior. Man, who is the glory of God, should not be veiled in the presence of God. However, the glory of man, the woman, should be veiled in God's presence.

The phrase "for this reason" (v. 10) is drawing a conclusion from the fact that woman is declared by the word of God to derive her origin from man and to have been created on his account. Because of this fact the woman is to have a "sign of authority on her head." Why is "authority" used here and to what does it refer?

Morna Hooker has summarized several varying interpretations of this difficult word. (See Morna D. Hooker, "Authority on her head: an examination of 1 Cor. xi.10," in NTS X, 1963–64, pp. 410–16.) She has noted that some see the term as a synonym for veil while others see it as referring to the protection that a veil gave to the Eastern woman. In this latter sense the wearing of the veil was seen to provide for the woman a place of dignity and authority. Another interpretation is that the word is a reference to a symbol of authority, and in this instance it is often interpreted to be the authority of the woman's husband, to whom she is obedient. Hooker herself feels that the veil is a symbol of new authority given to the woman to pray and to prophesy in worship. This was a power not given to the woman in Jewish life (or custom) and the Christian woman thus enjoyed a new privilege. The difficulty with her interpretation is that the context speaks of the subordination of the woman to the man, and the wearing of the veil must be understood in this context. Thus, the woman ought to wear on her head a veil as a sign of the power under which she has been placed. This is the power of the man, her husband. It would be possible in the case of an unmarried woman to see her wearing a veil at worship to show her subordination to her father or guardian, although this point is not immediately in Paul's mind.

Paul provides a further reason for the wearing of the veil by his reference to the "angels" in verse 10. Some have understood this as referring to bad angels who might lust against unveiled women in the spirit of Genesis 6:2. It is more likely that Paul is speaking of good angels who serve men (Heb. 1:14) and who would be especially present during worship. Women are called on to wear the veil for more reason than what the men and women in the congregation would see and think. The angels of God would notice what the woman did, and she should not present herself in a shocking manner before them.

Paul's basic principle in this passage is that the glory of God must not be covered in the presence of God and His angels. Hence, man must pray with uncovered head. However, the woman is the glory of man. Such glory must be covered in the presence of God and His angels lest it turn to shame. Hooker notes that:

> Although Paul's argument is based upon theological premises, it may perhaps reflect practical expediency; it is likely that it was the men of Corinth, rather than the angels, who were attracted by the women's uncovered locks, and that it was in this way that attention was being diverted from the worship of God (p. 415).

E. A Caution Concerning a Wrong Conclusion (11:11–12)

It might be possible for Paul's readers to infer too much from his presentation. It is not Paul's intention to lead them to think that woman is inferior to man, and he moves to qualify his previous words. Paul states that man and woman each owe their existence to the other and cannot continue without the other. Both man and woman owe their existence to God.

Paul's words in verse 11 would be a corrective to a haughty male boastfulness. He asserts that there is a partnership between the sexes, and in the Lord neither exists without the other. Man and woman are interdependent. Barrett says, "Together they make a unity in which each member is essential." Their mutual dependence is evident in ordinary life, but it will especially be seen in their mutual spiritual dependence where both are one in Christ Jesus (Gal. 3:28). It is Paul's conviction that Christians who live in the era when the present age and the age to come overlap should respect the ordinances of both ages.

Paul states in verse 12 that woman originally sprang from man. Since that time, however, man has come into existence through woman. The entire universe owes its existence to God. The man and the woman are not independent beings, but each finds usefulness and importance through a relationship with God that enhances their relationship with one another.

F. An Appeal to Their Sense of Propriety (11:13–15)

Paul has previously appealed to the ordinances of creation; he now appeals to social convention and distinctions of nature. In his presentation he speaks to the spiritual common sense of his readers.

The standards of propriety and convention do change from time to time and from place to place. However, in the cultural milieu with which Paul was most familiar it was not normally seen as proper for a woman to appear in public with an uncovered head. It was still less proper for a woman to pray to God with an uncovered head. Paul invites his readers to discern for themselves whether a woman should pray with an uncovered head, and he assumes that the answer is negative (v. 13). He is here calling for a scrupulous practice of social customs where those customs are not contrary to Christian commitment (Bruce).

In verses 14 and 15 Paul suggests that the instinctive judgments of nature would make it improper for man to have long hair. If a woman has this, however, it is her glory. Paul wrote from a background in which a man's wearing long hair was contrary to the custom of the Jews and the Greeks. The term "nature" is thus a reference to custom insofar as it conforms to the will of God. Based on the culture in which Paul was living, it made sense to assume that a man should have short hair and a woman long hair. Bruce notes that long hair in men was generally seen as effeminate but in a woman it was her pride. Barrett feels that the horror of homosexuality is behind much of Paul's argument in this section.

It is significant to observe in this section that Paul sees Christianity as respecting and refining the normal and the customary. While fanaticism would defy the customary, Christianity seeks to accommodate itself to that which does not involve compromise. Paul reflects a conviction that whatever shocked the common feelings of mankind would not likely be right.

G. An Appeal to the Custom of the Churches (11:16)

Paul was not disposed to argue the matter any further. In dealing with a church like the one in Corinth, which showed tendencies toward contentiousness, Paul has argued patiently and thoroughly for the foregoing customs. Now he states that he himself allowed no other custom than calling for women to pray with covered heads. And every other church did the same. Corinth sometimes displayed a tendency to be a law unto itself, and Paul indicated that the universal custom in all Christian churches demanded that a woman have her head covered while she prayed.

Paul's teachings in this passage about the role and attire of women are related partly to the customs of the day—but not fully so. Paul took care to ground some of his directions (vv. 7–10) in the divine order of creation. Thus, Christians today should not rapidly toss aside all that Paul here advises.

Paul does suggest that women are subordinated in function or role to men (v. 3), but he quickly moves to indicate that this does not imply inferiority (vv. 11–12). Men and women are seen spiritually as equals, as partners, and as mutually dependent. This was a new role for the Christian woman and a direct outcome of her Christian experience.

The enduring principle from Paul's directives is that both men and women should carefully preserve the distinctions of the sexes established by God. Both men and women must always dress and act in a becoming manner so as not to shock the customs of the time. The man must not seek to lord it over the woman with an aggressive heavy-handedness, and the woman must not rebel defiantly at the man's leadership in the home. Paul's discussion of the reciprocal roles of husbands and wives in Ephesians 5:22–33 further clarifies his presentation here.

This passage is taken as the basis for the insistence by some today that women wear hats in churches. In Paul's day the wearing of a veil or covering indicated the subordination of the wife to the husband. A woman's wearing a hat would not convey this meaning in twentieth-century America. Since the custom of covering the head of a female today lacks the symbolism that it had in the first century, the custom need not be seen as mandated by Scripture. A wife today may wear a hat if she desires, but she should not feel that the Bible commands such an action.

In this section Paul has generally kept in view the relation between man and woman as seen in marriage. He is primarily speaking of husband and wife. It would not be proper to take his words as the basis for calling on all women to manifest an abject submission to the male sex. Paul has the Christian home in mind as he writes.

For Further Study

1. Read the article on "Veil" in *The Zondervan Pictorial Bible Dictionary*.

2. Read again the exegesis of 11:3–9 and summarize in a sentence how Paul's advice would apply to the rebellious wife who minimizes the role of the husband in the family.

3. Read again the exegesis of 11:11 and 12 and summarize in a sentence how Paul's advice would apply to the chauvinistic husband who magnifies his leadership in the home so as to undermine the role of his wife.

Chapter 7

The Proper Observance of the Lord's Supper
(1 Corinthians 11:17–34)

In most Christian services today the observance of the Lord's Supper is a time of solemn worship dedicated to the memory of Christ's work on the cross. To Christians with that background the following passages seem puzzling, for the Lord's Supper in Corinth was an affair far from worshipful and was not dignified or edifying.

In the early days of Christianity the observance of the Lord's Supper took place in connection with a common meal often called a love feast (Jude 12). This meal was an imitation of the Last Supper, and the specific partaking of bread and wine was done during this meal. Christians joyously welcomed such opportunities for fellowship from their beginning (Acts 2:46), but in Corinth the intended harmony had degenerated to a social separation that was spiritually bankrupt.

To counter this difficulty, Paul focused in 11:17–22 on the specific abuse of the Lord's Supper in Corinth. To correct this abuse, he reminded the Corinthians that sharing the Lord's Supper was a memorial and an anticipation of the Lord Jesus (11:23–26) and that the Supper was not to be a time of social clannishness but a time of spiritual praise (11:27–34).

A. Abuse of the Supper (11:17–22)

Paul had concluded one charge to the Corinthian Church concerning its assembly for worship (11:2–10). He now moved to another concern of worship that was far more serious than the question of head covering. He could not approach this subject with any pleasure, for the church was worthy of blame and not praise (v. 17). The observance of class distinctions during the Lord's Supper had turned the fellowship meal into a harmful occasion. Instead of serving to quicken the spiritual life of Christians these services led to misconduct and suffering.

In verse 18 Paul amplifies the nature of the disturbance that has concerned him. There was schism in the church. Although the word for schism or division is the same as that found in 1:10, it is likely that the divisions are centered around social classes rather than personalities. Paul had learned of this division from either Chloe's people or his recent visitors from Corinth (16:17). As astounding as such news was, he was prepared to believe it because the informants were credible people, and he had a conviction that such developments would occur before the end. The exact nature of the social disturbance is more fully amplified in verses 21 and 22.

Paul philosophically accepts the inevitability of heresies (v. 19). The word for "differences" or "factions" refers to those who have chosen to follow a group of opinions. There is nothing derogatory about this unless it is self-willed. Paul is saying that unless there are factions, the genuine will not be distinguished from the rest. The genuine will be those whose behavior marks them as true Christians. In stating the necessity of factions Paul is not being resigned or ironic. He felt that the appearance of different groups in a church would cause the trusted and the true to be recognized in this life as an anticipation of the final decision of the judgment day. The mature and the stable would manifest themselves in the interests of unity and spiritual progress.

The Corinthians might well meet together to consume a meal, but such a meal brought no honor to the Lord Jesus Christ (v. 20). The term "Lord's Supper" is a reference to the actual meal that was eaten. During the course of the meal the bread and wine would be shared among the members as a memorial to the death of Christ. It is this sharing of the bread and fruit of the vine that is commonly called the Lord's Supper today. Paul had earlier warned that the table of the Lord could be profaned by idolatry (10:21). He now points out that a meal in honor of the Lord cannot be eaten in an atmosphere of social discrimination. Such a meal could "be profaned by faction as certainly as by idolatry" (Bruce).

The explanation of why this was not a meal in honor of the Lord is given in verse 21. The Lord's Supper in New Testament Corinth was a meal to which the participants brought food. The intention was that food and drink were to be moderately consumed by both rich and poor. The rich who brought much food were to share their resources with those who had brought little or none. Instead of sharing in a common meal the Corinthians participated in an undignified and gluttonous scramble. The wealthy ate and drank what they had brought and overindulged. The poor stood around with empty stomachs growling and glared enviously at their indulgent companions. There was no pretense at real sharing. Morris points out that such common meals in which the rich shared with the poor were sometimes a part of heathen religious practices. The shame was that the Corinthians did not even attain the standards of the heathen.

Paul addresses a forceful rebuke to the Corinthians in verse 22. If the Corinthians wanted to engage in this gluttonous practice, they were to do it in their own homes, for their actions constituted an insult to the church of God. The Corinthians were treating a fellowship meal as a time for unbridled indulgence, and this would serve as an embarrassment to those who were in need. Some members of the Corinthian church may have sought praise for the church by representing it in the most favorable light. Paul sternly responds that he can give them no praise for their inconsiderate, self-centered actions.

Paul's ideal for the observance of the Lord's Supper is that the church must reach out to include the rich, the poor, the prominent, and the outcast within a circle of love. Such a goal became a reality for many churches in the New Testament era and was a magnetic attraction to pull outsiders into a fellowship that offered warmth and acceptance, and to replace the loneliness and rejection of contemporary society. Churches today must create such a loving fellowship as a display of the power of Christianity amidst the divisive and fragmenting tendencies of the twentieth-century's lonely culture.

B. Meaning and Significance of the Lord's Supper (11:23–26)

Paul begins verse 23 with "For I." The presence of this emphatic pronoun leads Morris to suggest that Paul had received a personal revelation from the Lord on this matter. There are many other references in Scripture that suggest that Paul had revelations made directly to him (Acts 18:9–10; 22:18; 23:11; and Gal. 1:12). The terms used could also suggest that Paul was receiving and passing on the traditions of the Christian body concerning the observance of the Lord's Supper. It is ironic that a feast which brings such encouragement and consolation to Christians would have been instituted on a night when human maliciousness reached its peak in the betrayal of the Savior. The bread was one of the thin cakes used for the paschal meal and would not be the equivalent of a modern loaf of bread.

There is reasonable certainty that 1 Corinthians was written before any of the Gospels. If this is so, this account of the institution of the Lord's Supper would be the earliest written record of any of the words of the Lord. This account does contain some features not appearing elsewhere, such as the command to continue the service "until he comes" (v. 26).

The observance of the Lord's Supper is described here in verses 24–26 and also in Matthew 26:26–29; Mark 14:22–25; and Luke 22:19–20. There are some variations in the different accounts, but all four accounts refer to the following: (1) taking the bread, (2) giving thanks, (3) breaking the bread, (4) the words, "This is my body," (5) the passing of the cup, and (6) the words "blood" and "covenant" if a disputed passage in Luke is kept.

In verse 24 the phrase "This is my body" suggests that the bread represents the body of Christ. In 5:7 Paul had spoken of Jesus as the new Christian Passover, and he makes the same point here. The Passover celebrated deliverance from slavery to liberty, from sorrow to joy, and Christ has effected a similar deliverance for believers. The command, "do this," is the sole record of a directive to continue the Supper. The meal is a memorial of Christ. It constitutes an effort to call to mind His sufferings and His person. The early Christians saw the Supper as a commemoration of Christ's Resurrection as well as His death, for they selected the first day of the week as the most common time for this memorial.

In verse 25 Paul understands Jesus to be saying that the shedding of His blood is the means of establishing the new covenant. The shed blood of Jesus replaced the entire Jewish sacrificial system by providing forgiveness of sins and opening the way for the action of the Holy Spirit in the heart of the believer. Such Old Testament verses as Exodus 24:8 and Jeremiah 31:31–34 were in the background of Jesus' use of the term "covenant" here and in the Gospels. Those who enter into a covenant with the Lord also enter into a covenant with one another and establish a covenant community. The sharing of the cup was not presented here as an activity for domestic meals, but as something to be experienced at gatherings of the church. Paul's description does not suggest that the Lord's Supper necessarily occurred at each church gathering, but it was a frequent occurrence.

The partaking of the Lord's Supper by use of the bread and the wine was an open proclamation of the death of Christ (v. 26). Bruce feels that the word "proclaim" is so strong that it demands a public narration of the death of Christ. Thus, the supper became an evangelistic instrument. The act is a memorial, but in another sense it is also an anticipation. It proclaims the start of the time of salvation and prays for the appearance of the complete fulfillment when Christ returns. The commemoration of the absent Christ by this service will end when the absent Christ returns.

The anticipatory character of the Lord's Supper is a feature absent from many contemporary observances of the event. In this Supper Christians remember and praise the Lord for His sacrifice, but they also anticipate His return. The memory of this dual purpose of the Supper can heighten the expectation of lethargic and earthbound Christians for the appearance of the Lord of Glory.

C. Manner in Which the Supper Should Be Taken (11:27–34)

In verse 27 Paul demands that anyone partaking of the Lord's Supper be in a fit moral and spiritual condition. To partake of the Supper in an unworthy manner is a reference to the conditions described in verse 21. One who consumes the Supper in a spirit of factiousness, greed, or gluttony contradicts the purpose of Christ's self-offering and shares the meal in an unworthy manner. Paul's description is that one who shares the Supper in this manner profanes it. The NEB suggests that such a person "will be guilty of desecrating the body and blood of the Lord." Paul is not suggesting that partaking of the Supper in an unworthy manner makes a person responsible for Christ's death. The greedy, selfish participant in the Lord's Supper prostitutes the very purpose of Christ's death for all mankind. In that sense he profanes and desecrates His death.

In verse 28 Paul indicates that a person who participates in the Lord's Supper must conduct a rigorous self-examination. The context suggests particularly that his self-examination must discern "whether or not he is living and acting 'in love and charity' with his neighbours" (Bruce). Paul is not suggesting that a man be morally faultless before he share in the meal, but he must be earnest and sincere in his own self-examination and commitment.

Paul provides a reason for his command that the participant examine himself by his explanation of verse 29. He demands that those who share in the meal understand their corporate unity in Christ. If some in Corinth consumed food in a gluttonous manner, they did not discern the body. In this verse the term "body" seems to be a reference to the church as the body of Christ. Paul is calling on his readers to recognize the fact that they have become one body in Christ (12:13) and to partake of the meal in recognition of that fellowship made possible through Christ. Those who fail to do this will receive condemnation. This is not a suggestion of eternal damnation but a form of punishment to be mentioned next.

The spiritual ills already mentioned cause physical results in verse 30. Some in the congregation at Corinth were in ill health, and some were asleep. Paul traces the cause back to their wrong attitude toward the solemn service of the Lord's Supper. Translators differ as to whether the term "asleep" in verse 30 describes Christians who have died or Christians who are spiritually asleep. In the light of the usage of the same word in 1 Thessalonians 4:13 the reference here is likely to physical death. Some have also traced the poor health to the results of excessive drinking mentioned in verse 21, but Paul is referring to the chastening hand of the Lord (v. 32).

In verses 31 and 32 Paul amplifies the benefits of individual self-judgment. Christians who examine themselves will escape the judgments and illnesses mentioned in verse 30. The verb translated "judged" in verse 31 calls for a true and penetrating self-examination, not a superficial glance. When Christians fail to exercise such self-judgment, God may judge them after the manner of verse 30. That judgment is still different from the condemnation given to the wicked, for it is God's chastisement, His effort to train and educate those whom He loves (Heb. 12:5–11). God brings this chastisement on His children "to preserve believers from being overwhelmed in the condemnation pronounced on the godless *world* (cf. Exod. 15:26)" (Bruce).

The conclusion of the entire discussion is given in verses 33 and 34. Instead of allowing the meal to become an example of selfish overeating, Christians should share their food and drink and give consideration to those who cannot contribute much food. If some were so hungry that they could not wait to share with their brothers in Christ, they should eat at home. Then they might come together for a time of fellowship rather than a time of selfish indulgence. Their meetings would be an experience of grace and not an occasion for judgment. Paul's last words in this chapter remind his readers that there are more matters he wants to set straight, but these can wait for his arrival, whenever that occurs.

Paul's stern warnings in this section are a reminder that participation in the Lord's Supper is no trivial matter. It is a solemn privilege to be undertaken by those who come in earnestness and commitment. The Supper is a memorial to Christ, an anticipation of His return, and it becomes a source of much help and encouragement to the participant. It should be undertaken only by a believer serious about his fellowship with God and other brothers in Christ. It must be preceded by rigorous self-examination and not be performed superficially at each quarterly, monthly, or weekly observance.

For Further Study

1. Read the article on "Lord's Supper" in *The Zondervan Pictorial Bible Dictionary*.

2. Read 11:23–28 and then list the personal spiritual benefits of observing the Lord's Supper.

3. State in a sentence what Paul means when he speaks of observing the Lord's Supper in an unworthy manner.

4. List several practical suggestions that your church might use to encourage the participation of Christians of different social classes in activities in your church.

Chapter 8

The Use of Spiritual Gifts

(1 Corinthians 12:1–14:40)

The New Testament gives great prominence to the Holy Spirit. Indeed, references to Him are found in every book except Philemon, and 2 and 3 John. And of all the writings of the New Testament, none is so full of teaching about the Spirit as are the epistles of Paul, where the Spirit is mentioned nearly 120 times. James Denney wrote that "to the men who wrote the New Testament and to those for whom they wrote, the Spirit was not a doctrine but an experience. . . . In some sense this covered everything that they included in Christianity" ("Holy Spirit," *Dictionary of Christ and the Gospels.* Ed. James Hastings).

Israel's prophets had predicted that the messianic age would be attended by a remarkable effusion of the Holy Spirit (cf. Joel 2:28ff.), and on the day of Pentecost Peter declared that the prophetic word had been fulfilled. It is not surprising that in time, disorders and problems arose. Some persons who were deluded or impostors claimed to be instruments of the Spirit; some envied those who in their opinion possessed superior gifts; and others, puffed up with pride, made an ostentatious display of their gifts. There are also indications that at least on occasion several persons clamored to exercise their gifts at the same time. Others focused their attention on the more spectacular ("showy") gifts (specifically, speaking in tongues) and deprecated the gifts that Paul considered the more useful. The result was envy, vanity, and division.

It was to correct such abuses that Paul wrote chapters 12–14. Chapter 12 contains a general survey of spiritual gifts, emphasizing their common origin, their remarkable diversity, and their one great purpose. Chapter 13 sets forth the practice of love as "the most excellent way." In 14:1–25 Paul deals specifically with the gift of tongues, contrasting it with the gift of prophecy and showing the superiority of the latter. The passage closes (14:26–33) with general directions concerning the conduct of church worship.

A. The Gifts of the Spirit[1]: A General Survey (12:1–31)

Among the questions raised in the Corinthians' letter to Paul was one that related to spiritual gifts (12:1a). Actually, this is the third of a series of questions relating to public worship, the former two having to do with the veiling of women (11:2–16) and the observance of the Lord's Supper (11:17–34). The wearing of the veil was essentially a matter of social decorum; the observance of the Supper, a matter of church fellowship. The gifts of the Spirit had to do with supernatural, mysterious, and personal experiences that touched the very life of the church.

Chapter 12, which gives a general survey of gifts, is foundational to the entire discussion of the topic. It falls into three distinct parts: (1) the test of speaking in the Spirit (vv. 1–3), (2) the diversity of spiritual gifts (vv. 4–11), and (3) the illustration of the body (vv. 12–31a).

1. *The test of speaking in the Spirit* (12:1–3)

The first verse introduces the topic to be discussed in chapters 12–14: "Now about spiritual gifts" (cf. 7:1; 8:1; et al.). There is no word for "gifts" in the Greek, but the context seems to require that this word be supplied. "I do not want you to be ignorant" is a deliberate understatement intended to heighten the effect. It is Paul's way of arresting the attention of his readers and saying to them that he definitely wants them to have accurate knowledge about spiritual gifts.

Verse 2 explains the need for the instruction that follows. Reference is made to the reader's pagan background ("you were pagans") and to their being "led astray" to the worship of "dumb [voiceless] idols." "Led astray" is the translation of a word that suggests being led away by force. The present tense is iterative, suggesting that it happened again and again. It pictures the Corinthians in their heathenism as swayed by blind, unintelligent impulse. They acted as persons "under constraint, as helpless, as men who [knew] no better" (Morris). We are not told who it was that led them in this fashion, but the allusion could be to Satan, "the wily wire-puller of moral mischief" (Evans). Conybeare thinks the context suggests pagans who claimed to possess special powers from the divinity: "You were blindly led astray to worship dumb and senseless idols (by those who pretended to have gifts from heaven)."

The adjective "dumb," meaning "voiceless" or "silent," points up that

---

[1]Spiritual gifts are not to be identified with natural endowments; they are to be understood as special capacities for service graciously bestowed by God on those who are in Christ.

the pagan deities were unable to answer those who called on them. Perhaps there is an intended contrast between the silence of the idols and the demon-inspired noise of their worshipers. "Somehow or other you were influenced" ("however you may have been moved," RSV) amplifies the earlier verb ("led astray").

The crucial test for deciding whether those who claimed to be under the influence of the Spirit were really so is stated in verse 3. "Therefore" introduces a conclusion: Since the Corinthians in the time of their heathenism were under the sway of evil spirits (v. 2), Paul felt it imperative to make known (Gr., gnōrizō, a rather solemn word, suggesting the importance of what follows) to them the truth about God's Spirit and the criterion for recognizing those who truly spoke under His influence. The test has to do with loyalty to Christ: "no one who is speaking by the Spirit of God says, 'Jesus be cursed,'[2] and no one can say, 'Jesus is Lord,' except by the Holy Spirit." Spirit-inspired speech always honors Christ. Therefore, not a mystical tongue but an intelligent confession of Jesus as Lord is the mark of one who truly speaks in the Spirit. As Barrett puts it, "Not the manner but the content of ecstatic speech determines its authenticity."

Paul's words imply that the specific problem bothering the Corinthians had to do with speaking in the Spirit. In their pagan experience they had been personally familiar with utterances made under the influence of some "spirit," and they doubtless knew of the wild ecstasies of the cult of Dionysius. Moreover, they knew that one who speaks in tongues may be unaware of what he is saying. These considerations (and perhaps others) led them to wonder whether everything spoken in ecstasy was good and whether it all came from God's Spirit. That questions such as these were being asked by the Corinthians seems to be corroborated by the fact that after the general treatment of spiritual gifts in chapter 12, the discussion focuses more and more on glossolalia and prophecy, both gifts of Spirit-inspired speech.

2. The diversity of gifts (12:4–11)

In these verses several matters concerning spiritual gifts—their common origin, their rich variety, their one purpose, their sovereign distribution—are interwoven to such an extent that it is difficult to make a continuous outline of the passage. However, the dominant thought is that

---

[2]Morris feels that a natural inference to be drawn from these words is that someone had actually called Jesus accursed. He adds that there was perhaps a connection with Paul's teaching that Jesus "was made a curse for us" (Gal. 3:13). "It is not beyond the bounds of possibility that some excitable and imperfectly instructed Corinthian had distorted the thought in an ecstatic utterance."

of diversity. This diversity is affirmed in verses 4–7, explained in verses 8–10, and summarized in verse 11.

a) *Diversity affirmed* (12:4–7)

The Spirit prompts all believers to confess that Jesus is Lord, but within the unity of faith there are "different kinds of gifts" (v. 4), "different kinds of service" (v. 5), and "different kinds of working" (v. 6). "Different kinds" is the translation of a word whose root expresses the idea of division. From this it comes to mean "apportionment" or "distribution," and this is the meaning preferred by some interpreters for this passage. Arndt and Gingrich, for instance, suggest the rendering "allotments of spiritual gifts," and so forth. However, they explain that "difference" or "variety" is also a possible meaning of the word in our text, and this is the meaning preferred in many commentaries. Barrett says the meaning of the word is "distribution," though the idea of "varieties" is implied. It is this implied idea that is used in most of the popular versions (KJV, ASV, RSV, NASB, NIV, etc.).

"Gifts" (Gr., *charismata*, built on the root word meaning "grace"), "service" (Gr., *diakoniai*, "services"), and "working" (Gr., *energēmata*, "activities," "operations")—these words, though representing different perspectives, all refer to the same thing. What is from one point of view a gracious bestowal (gift) by the Spirit is from another a service (ministration), and from still another an operation of power (working). These then are not separate classes of spiritual things but varied names for them. "Gifts" (*charismata*, "grace-gifts") calls attention to their quality and ground (i.e., that they are a free bounty of God, not bestowed as a reward for human effort or seeking); "service" (*diakoniai*) emphasizes their purpose, how they are to be used; "working" (*energēmata*) points to the power operative in them.

That the distribution of these gifts proceeds from "the same Spirit," "the same Lord," and "the same God" suggests at least two lessons: One is that there is within this abundant variety a profound unity. The other is that since the gifts come from the same source they should not be the occasion for rivalry, discontent, or feelings of superiority.

Verse 7 serves three purposes. First, it asserts that to every believer a "manifestation of the Spirit" is given; the gifts, therefore, are not the special privilege of a few outstanding persons. On each believer some gift is bestowed. This gift is a "manifestation of the Spirit" in the sense that it manifests the presence of the Spirit among God's people. Findlay comments that "these charisms, blossoming out in rich, changeful variety, disclose the potencies of the Spirit ever dwelling in the church." The MLB uses the word "evidence" instead of "manifestation." Second, by affirm-

ing that each believer's gift is a "manifestation of the Spirit," the verse
tacitly rebukes those Corinthians who were attaching a special importance to the particular gifts they possessed. Third, the verse affirms that
just as these diverse gifts have a single source, so also they have the same
purpose: all are intended "for the common good" (RSV) of the church.
Barrett translates it, "with a view to mutual benefit."

b) *Diversity explained* (12:8–10)

Having affirmed the diversity of spiritual gifts, Paul now explains what
this diversity is. "This," he seems to say, "is how this diversity works."
Then follows a list of nine of the manifestations of the Spirit.[3] Attempts to
group them often smack of artificiality and are seldom satisfactory. Some
interpreters have suggested a threefold classification: gifts associated with
the intellect (v. 8), gifts related to the will (vv. 9, 10a), and gifts associated
with the feelings or emotions (v. 10b). (Compare the punctuation of the
ASV.) Others have suggested a fivefold arrangement: (1) gifts having to do
with intellectual power ("message of wisdom," "message of knowledge");
(2) gifts expressing miraculous power ("faith," "healings," and "miracles"); (3) gifts that relate to teaching power ("prophecy"); (4) gifts that
pertain to critical power ("distinguish between spirits"); and (5) those
having to do with ecstatic powers ("kinds of tongues," "interpretation of
tongues"). Hodge concludes that the "principle of classification is not
discernible." The RSV, NIV, and others punctuate in such a way that no
divisions into classes are indicated. They appear to represent a correct
understanding of the passage. However, it is significant that gifts of intelligent and thoughtful utterance are listed first and that the gifts of ecstatic
utterance and interpretation are listed last.

The "message of wisdom" is the gift of communicating wisdom. "Message of knowledge" is the gift of communicating knowledge. Barrett sees
both of these as having to do with "instructive discourse" and points out
that it is not clear how (or whether) they are to be distinguished. He
concludes that Paul may refer to the same thing in both phrases, varying
his language as in verses 4–6. If a distinction is made, "message of
wisdom" may speak of practical discourse, "message of knowledge" of the
ability to expound Christian truth. Observe also that these gifts emphasize not wisdom or knowledge *per se* but their "utterance" character. As
Barrett puts it, "It is the discourse, not the wisdom or knowledge behind

---

[3]There are four passages in the New Testament that list spiritual gifts: 1 Corinthians
12:8–10, 28–30; Romans 12:3–8; Ephesians 4:11; 1 Peter 4:10–11. That no two listings are
alike shows that no passage names all the gifts. Moreover, the differences may suggest that
God gave the specific gifts needed by the several congregations.

it, that is the spiritual gift, for it is this that is of direct service to the church." What Paul values is wisdom and knowledge *communicated*, that is, spoken, for the common good of the church.

"Faith" cannot be saving faith, for all Christians have this. It must therefore be wonder-working faith (cf. 13:2). "Miraculous powers" ("workings of miracles," ASV) apparently include more than "gifts of healings," since the two terms are distinguished. We may infer from this that some believers had the specific gift of healing the sick, while others had more general miracle-working power (cf., the raising of Dorcas or Tabitha [Acts 9:40], the smiting of Elymas with blindness [Acts 13:11], etc.). "Prophecy" is the gift of speaking for God under the immediate inspiration of the Spirit (cf. Agabus [Acts 11:28; 21:10f.] and Philip's daughters [Acts 21:9]).[4] To "distinguish between spirits" was the gift that enabled a person to distinguish whether a person spoke under divine inspiration, from the impulse of his own mind, or under the influence of an evil spirit (cf. 1 Thess. 5:20–21). Some interpreters think "kinds of tongues" may include the ability to speak known languages miraculously (cf. Acts 2:2ff.) as well as the gift of ecstatic utterance. However, what is said about "tongues" in chapter 14 seems to support the view that "kinds of tongues" refers only to ecstatic speech, that is, utterances not understood by speakers or hearers apart from the help of someone with the gift of "interpretation of tongues." The meaning attached to the latter gift will depend on one's conception of the gift of tongues.

c) *Diversity summarized* (12:11)

There is nothing really new in this verse. It only emphasizes things either said or implied in the preceding verses: the common origin of all the gifts ("All these are the work[5] of one and the same Spirit"); the possession by every Christian of some gift ("gives them to each one"); and the sovereignty of the Spirit in the distribution of the gifts ("as he determines [wills]"). Christians should earnestly desire the greater gifts (12:31), but in the final analysis it is God's Spirit who determines who is to have this or that gift.

---

[4]Berkhof writes that in his opinion "prophecy is the gift of understanding and expressing what the will of God is for a given present situation" (*Doctrine of the Holy Spirit*, p. 91). F. D. Bruner thinks such terms as "thoughtful speech," "testimony," or even "counsel" are better translations for the Greek word "rendered now somewhat archaically 'prophecy.'" His feeling is that "committees often manifest this gift," adding that "it is often only in committee meetings that the *charismata* given the church members have the opportunity of expression" (p. 297). See comments on verse 28.

[5]The Greek word is *energei*, from which we get "energize." It "suggests that the Spirit is the source of boundless and manifold energy and power" (Barrett).

3. *The illustration of the body* (12:12–31a)

The preceding paragraph (vv. 4–11) has emphasized the great diversity of gifts bestowed by the Spirit on the people of God. The present passage (vv. 12–31a), by use of the analogy of the many parts that make up the human body, will stress that this diversity contributes to the essential oneness of the church. "Differentiation," writes Findlay, "is the essence of bodily life. The unity of the Church is not that of inorganic nature—a monotonous aggregation of similars, as in a pool of water or a heap of stones; it is the oneness of a living organism, no member of which exercises the same faculty as another."

Five lessons may be drawn from Paul's analogy:

a) *The church is, like the human body, one* (12:12–13).

That is to say, it is an organic whole. Verse 12 states this fact: "The [human] body is a unit, . . . so it is with Christ." We would expect this to read, ". . . so also is the church," and that is the idea. "Christ stands by metonymy for the community united through Him and grounded in Him" (Heinrici, quoted by Findlay). Since the church is the body of Christ, "Christ himself may be said to be a body made up of many members" (Barrett).

What is *stated* in verse 12 is *confirmed* in the verse following: "For we were [the word is emphatic] all baptized by one Spirit into one body—whether Jews or Greeks, slave or free—and we were all given the one Spirit to drink." Through baptism in/by the Spirit *all* believers have become members of Christ's body. The emphasis is on the *oneness* of all who are in Christ—whether they are Jews or Greeks, slaves or free men. The Greek expression translated "by one Spirit" should be understood as a locative construction, denoting the sphere (element) of the action, not its agency. A comparison of this verse with Matthew 3:11; Mark 1:8; Luke 3:16; and John 1:33 suggests that Christ is the baptizer. "Were . . . baptized" refers to "a definite act in the past, probably to the inward experience of the Holy Spirit symbolized by the act of baptism" (Robertson). It is the experience of every believer ("we . . . all"); therefore Christians are never commanded in the New Testament to be baptized in (with/by) the Spirit. Gould says the baptism referred to is water baptism, but it is thought of "not merely as an outward act in water; it has a spiritual side, the outward rite symbolizing an inward, spiritual reality. And just as the body is baptized in water, so the soul is baptized in the Spirit of God." Bruce, who sees the matter differently, explains that "faith-union with Christ brought his people into membership of the Spirit-baptized community, procuring for them the benefits of the once-for-all outpouring of the Spirit at the dawn of the new age, while baptism in water was retained as the outward and visible sign of the incorporation 'into Christ' (cf. Gal.

3:27)." Stott says that the verbs "baptized" and "given to drink" must both "be taken as an allusion, not just to the Pentecost event, but also to its blessing personally received by all Christians at their conversion." The two verbs probably describe the same experience under different figures. Findlay speaks of it as "an outward affusion and an inward absorption." Believers are at once *"immersed in"* and *"saturated with* the Spirit." Similarly, Barrett comments that "the Spirit not only surrounds us but is within us."

b) *The church is, like the human body, made up of many members* (12:14–20)

Its unity, affirmed in verses 12 and 13, does not consist in its being one member but in the unification of its many members. Verse 14 makes the general statement that "the body is not made up of one part, but many." Verses 15 and 16, mentioning the foot and the hand, the ear and the eye, illustrate by giving specific instances of this general statement. Verses 17 and 18 expand on this by showing that each of the diverse members is necessary for the completeness of the body. Hearing, as well as seeing and smelling, are needed functions of the one body.[6] Verse 19 teaches that diversity is essential to the very being of the body. Without the many members "there would be no body at all, but only a single monstrous limb" (Findlay). Verse 20, which is made more forceful in Greek by the absence of a verb, concisely summarizes the essence of everything said in verses 12–19: "As it is, there are many parts, but one body." This is true both of the human body and of the church.

c) *The members of the church, with their diverse gifts, are, like the parts of the body, mutually dependent* (12:21–24)

As in the body the eye needs the hand and the head needs the feet, so in the church the more highly gifted members are as dependent on those less favored as the latter are on the former.

d) *All the members are to have a fellow-feeling* (12:25–26)

God's purpose in so constituting things was "that there should be no division in the body, but that its parts should have equal concern for each other" (v. 25). "Division," when used in a context like this, suggests alienation of feeling, manifestations of jealousy or scorn. Goodspeed uses the word "clash"; RSV, "discord."

The statement of the last half of verse 25 is the opposite of "division." God's intention is that each member have an anxious solicitude for the other members. In the human body God has so arranged things that the eye is as concerned for the welfare of the foot as it is for its own well-

---

[6]Verse 18 contains an additional principle, namely, that the place and gifts of each member of the church are determined by the Lord.

being; this, it is implied, is God's desire for the church as well. When this is the case, the suffering of one member is shared by all, and the honor that another receives brings joy to all.

e) *Each believer is a part of the body of Christ, and no one is self-sufficient* (12:27–31a)

The description of the human body (vv. 12–26) is applicable to the church (vv. 27–31a). This is stated in verse 27: "Now you are the body of Christ, and each one of you is a part of it ['. . . and everyone has his place in it,' Beck]."

Verses 28–31a contain a list of eight kinds of members. It has features that are similar to as well as features that are different from the list of nine "manifestations of the Spirit" in verses 8–10. For example, both lists place "tongues" and "interpretation of tongues" last. But there is an overall emphasis on rank that is unique to this list. Moreover, the members/manifestations enumerated in the two lists are not parallel to one another. Neither list is intended to be exhaustive.

"Apostles," listed first, were confined to the first century. They were commissioned as Christ's representatives and sent forth with His authority. "Prophets" were those who spoke under the immediate inspiration of the Spirit. They were primarily instruments of divine revelation. Barrett says their ministry "was directed in the main to the requirements of the moment rather than to the enunciation of permanent principles." Some of their functions were similar to those of present-day preachers, others were different (cf. Acts 11:27ff.). (For additional comments see the discussion of "prophecy" at v. 10.) After the New Testament writings came into general circulation, the need for apostles and prophets ceased, and with the cessation of the need the offices ceased also.

The function of the teacher was to give instruction in the Old Testament Scriptures and the teachings of Jesus. That is to say, the teacher served not to make fresh revelations of truth, but to impress on the mind and apply to life the truth already revealed.

On "miracles" and "gifts of healings," see verse 9. Those who "help others" denotes those specially gifted to render assistance to others, whether the poor, the sick, the discouraged, or church officers. "Administrators" ("organizers," Phillips) speaks of those with the gift of administration, those who directed the affairs of the church. The Greek word is built on a root that denotes a steersman, a pilot. "Wise guides" (*Basic Bible*) is therefore a felicitous rendering. On "kinds of tongues," see verse 10.

Verses 29 and 30 imply that no one has all the gifts. The questions ("Are all apostles?" etc.) expect the answer "No." They might be worded, "All are not apostles, are they?" and so forth.

All cannot have every gift, but it is appropriate to desire earnestly (i.e., be ambitious to acquire) the greater gifts, that is, those that are more useful (v. 31a). This appeal teaches that there are not only differences in the gifts, but that some of them have greater usefulness within the body. Furthermore, it reveals that even though the gifts are distributed by the sovereign will of the Spirit (v. 11) it is not wrong to desire these greater gifts. The present tense of the verb suggests the rendering, "Continue to desire." "The Corinthians," comment Robertson and Plummer, "coveted the greater gifts, but they had formed a wrong estimate as to which were the greater."

Verse 31b, which introduces the theme of the next chapter, suggests that there is something better than yearning for gifts, even the best of them. "A still more excellent way" (RSV) is love, a "fruit of the Spirit" (not a spiritual gift) that is open to all (cf. Gal. 5:22). The gifts do not necessarily make one a better Christian, but love will. Love will also help one to recognize (and desire) the best gifts, and will prompt one to use them effectively.

B. The Practice of Love: The Most Excellent Way (13:1–13)

Though often read and studied in isolation from its context, this chapter is vitally connected with chapters 12 and 14. The former speaks in the main of the rich variety of spiritual gifts, the latter of the proper use of those gifts. Chapter 13 is intended to teach that it is love alone that safeguards the use (ch. 14) of that which the Spirit has so richly provided (ch. 12). Harnack describes this passage as "the greatest, strongest, deepest thing Paul ever wrote" (quoted by Robertson and Plummer).

The word used for "love" in this chapter is one of the three basic terms for love in the Greek language. It is instructive to compare them. One term is *erōs*, which essentially denotes sexual desire. It speaks of the love of passion, of lust. It is self-centered and grasping, ever seeking its own satisfaction. Because of the base associations of this word, it was never used in the New Testament. The second word is *philia*, meaning affection or friendship between kindred spirits. The noun occurs only once in the New Testament (James 4:4), but the verb (found in a number of passages) is used of love of family, the Father's love for the Son, Christ's love for Lazarus, God's love for His people, man's love for God. The third word, *agapē*, is the one used in the present passage. Because it was practically unknown in nonbiblical Greek, Trench calls it a word born within the bosom of revealed religion. The verb form (*agapaō*) was used in secular writings, but it had a connotation that was somewhat cold and colorless. "Esteem" might best express its meaning. The New Testament writers, however, took this word and gave it a full, rich meaning. They made it, in fact, the distinctive New Testament word for love. It has nothing to do with lust, nor is it mere affection. It is self-giving love, involving the direction of the will.

There is little or no disagreement among·interpreters as to the structure of the passage. It falls naturally into three clearly marked parts: verses 1–3, which set forth the necessity of love; verses 4–7, which show the excellence of love; and verses 8–13, which affirm the perpetuity of love.

1. *The necessity of love* (13:1–3)

Robertson and Plummer summarize as follows: "The one indispensable gift is Love. If one were to have all the special gifts in the highest perfection, without having Love, one would produce nothing, be nothing, and gain nothing."

One thing that stands out conspicuously in these verses is the repetition of "if" (used five times) and "all" ("all mysteries," "all knowledge," "all faith," "all I possess"). Paul uses these expressions to depict a person of remarkable qualities—"one who has matchless eloquence, profound insight, wide knowledge, tremendous faith, [and] the will to utmost sacrifice" (Scroggie, p. 31). Another significant phrase is "but have not love," found three times (vv. 1,2,3). The point is that "though all of these qualities were found in a single person, if he were without love, what he did would profit him nothing, and he himself would be nothing" (Scroggie, p. 31).

Love is necessary to the meaningful use of the gift of tongues: "If I speak in the tongues of men and of angels, but have not love, I am only a resounding gong or a clanging cymbal" (v. 1). Paul might have written, "If *you* should speak . . .," but in using himself as the illustration of failure, he sets an example of love and humility.

In the previous listings of gifts, tongues and their interpretation were mentioned last. The fact that speaking in tongues is mentioned first in this chapter lends support to the view that an overemphasis on this gift was at the heart of the problem under discussion. Paul asserts that even the use of tongues of the most exalted character, unaccompanied by love, is worthless. The reference to "resounding gong" and "a clanging cymbal" brings to mind the image of a person who is all sound and noise, having no real worth.

Love is necessary to the effective use of the gift of prophecy (v. 2a). This gift had to do with knowing and declaring the will of God. The mention of "all mysteries" and "all knowledge" in close connection with "prophecy" implies that these are at least sometimes involved in the exercise of the gift of prophecy. That is to say, knowing mysteries and possessing knowledge are not additional to the prophetic gift, but are a part of it. Rigid distinctions in the meanings of "mysteries" and "knowledge" probably should not be made. Paul was likely piling up words for rhetorical effect: "If I know everything there is to know."[7]

Love is necessary to the value of faith (v. 2b). Faith here must mean wonder-working faith, as is indicated by the addition of the words "that I can move mountains" (cf. 12:9). To "move mountains" was a proverbial expression for a great miracle.

Love is necessary to make deeds of mercy and sacrifice meaningful (v. 3). Such acts as bestowing one's goods to feed the poor or giving one's life in martyrdom may do some good. But, if not motivated by love, they are of no benefit to the one performing these acts. The language clearly implies that it is possible for such deeds to be done from some motive other than love. Scroggie remarks that "the pages of Christian history show that men will fight and die for Christianity, who will not live in its spirit, which is love" (p. 30).

2. The excellence of love (13:4–7)

These verses are not so much a description of love as a depiction of love in action. They personify love, showing what it does, what it does not do, and the ways in which it manifests itself. In this manner the apostle extols the virtues of love and shows it to be of surpassing worth. There is an implied contrast between love's behavior and the behavior of those who placed inordinate value on spectacular gifts.

There are few exegetical problems here. A summary treatment, calling attention to the various traits of love, may be sufficient. There seems to be no special, logical order in the listing of the qualities of love. They were apparently enumerated simply as they occurred to the apostle, and in contrast to the deformities of character that the Corinthians exhibited.

Verse 4. Love is patient, that is, it is long-tempered, not quick to take offense or to inflict punishment. Love is kind ("plays the gentle part," Robertson and Plummer). The Greek word, found only in Christian writings, conveys the thought of being loving and merciful. Its position in relation to "is patient" suggests that the disposition of kindness is the positive counterpart of patience. Love does good to those who do harm. Love does not envy. C. B. Williams renders it, "Love never boils with

---

[7]A "mystery" was a secret truth undiscoverable apart from revelation by God. If "knowledge" is to be distinguished from it, perhaps we could say that "knowledge" here denotes general knowledge, of which the understanding of mysteries was a specific part.

jealousy." The Greek word may express any wrong feeling, particularly jealousy and envy, "excited in view of the good of others" (Hodge). Love *does not boast.* This suggests that there is no ostentation about love. Robertson and Plummer understand the verb to mean "does not play the braggart"; Moffatt, "makes no parade"; Phillips, love is not "anxious to impress." *Is not proud,* is the translation of a Greek verb used frequently in 1 Corinthians (4:6, 18–19; 5:2; 8:1), and means that love is not conceited or arrogant. Goodspeed understands it to mean that love "does not put on airs"; Phillips, that it does not "cherish inflated ideas of its own importance."

Verse 5. The statement that love *is not rude* may mean that love "does not treat anybody unfairly" (Barrett) or "does nothing of which one ought to be ashamed" (Hodge). Moffatt uses the expression, "is never rude"; the MLB has "unmannerly." Robertson and Plummer explain it to mean that "Love is tactful, and does nothing that would raise a blush." *It is not self-seeking* means that "Love does not insist on its own way" (RSV). *Is not easily angered* means love is not irritable or touchy, is not quick to take offense. Robertson and Plummer interpret it to mean that love "is not embittered by injuries." *Keeps no record of wrongs* means that love does not harbor resentment, does not bear malice.

Verse 6. Love *does not delight in evil.* That is to say, it does not take pleasure in the wrongdoing committed by others, "is never glad when others go wrong" (Moffatt). On the contrary, love *rejoices with the truth.* Weymouth translates it, "joyfully sides with the truth"; C. B. Williams puts it, "always glad when truth prevails." The thought is that love does not sympathize with evil but with goodness.

Verse 7. Love *always protects* (ASV: "beareth all things"). Hodge takes this to mean that love "bears in silence all annoyances and troubles." Barrett observes that the Greek verb normally means "to endure," but prefers to understand it here in the sense of "support." "Love," he explains, "is the support of the world." The statement that love *always trusts* (ASV: "believeth all things") may mean that love is not suspicious, that is, it "readily credits what men say in their own defence" (Hodge). This does not mean that the loving person is gullible, but "in doubtful cases he will prefer being too generous in his conclusions to suspecting another unjustly" (Robertson and Plummer). Barrett sees a different idea in Paul's words, interpreting them to mean that love "never loses faith." Love *always hopes,* that is, "hopes under all circumstances" (MLB). That love *always perseveres* means that love perseveres under the assaults of persecution, suffering, and other adversities. Barrett comments that "no hardship or rebuff ever makes love cease to be love."

3. *The perpetuity of love* (13:8–13)

In contrast with spiritual gifts, which are for time alone, love will go on manifesting itself throughout time and eternity. The gifts are bestowed for a purpose, and when they have served that purpose, they will cease to be. The leading idea of this unit is expressed in its opening statement: "Love never fails" (v. 8a). The verb literally means "to fall," but it is capable of numerous renderings. Here Arndt and Gingrich understand it to have the sense of failing, becoming invalid, coming to an end. Barrett observes that "if my relationship with my fellow-man is soured by his rebuffs, then it is not love; genuine love will always persist." At its deepest level Paul's assertion can be made only about God's love.

The remainder of verse 8 contrasts the permanence of love with the transitoriness of three gifts, the three apparently representing all the gifts. *Prophecies* "will cease" (*katargēthēsontai*, v. 8b). The idea is that prophecy, having served its purpose, will be brought to an end. *Tongues* "will be stilled" (*pausontai*, v. 8c). The verb is different from that used in reference to prophecies, but Arndt and Gingrich give it essentially the same meaning: "will come to an end," that is, cease. *Knowledge* "will pass away," be brought to an end (*katargēthēsetai*, v. 8d). Barrett, who takes "knowledge" to mean secret information about God, interprets Paul to mean that "when God manifests himself at large no man can boast about his secret stock of knowledge." Morris explains that "knowledge" denotes "the painfully acquired knowledge of earthly things." There will be no place for such knowledge "in the light of the immediate knowledge of God."

Verses 9 and 10 explain (note "For" at the beginning of v. 9) why prophecies and knowledge will cease. They are fragmentary and imperfect. Therefore, "when perfection comes, the imperfect disappears" (v. 10). "Knowledge and prophecy are useful as lamps in the darkness, but they will be useless when the eternal Day has dawned" (Robertson and Plummer). Some interpreters take "perfection" to be a reference to the canon of Scripture, but there is nothing in the context to suggest this meaning. Barrett understands it to mean the totality, the whole truth of God (in contrast to that which is partial and fragmentary). Robertson and Plummer see in the clause a reference to the consummation of God's purpose. Ultimately the idea is about the same in the last two interpretations. "The Apostle is saying nothing about the cessation of [charismata] in this life: prophesyings and knowledge might always be useful. All he asserts is, that these things will have no use when completeness is revealed; and therefore they are inferior to Love" (Robertson and Plum-

mer). "Disappears" comes from the same verb used twice already in verse
8 (*katargēomai*).

Verse 11 confirms, by way of an appeal to personal experience, what
has been said about the incomplete and transitory character of spiritual
gifts. Implied is the thought that "all the spiritual gifts belong to the state
of spiritual childhood, but when Christ comes, and maturity is reached,
they will no longer be needed, and so will be put away" (Scroggie, p. 68).

Verse 12 confirms ("Now"; in ASV, "For") the illustration of verse 11.
What childhood is to manhood, so is the present life to the life to come.
The reference to seeing "a poor reflection" (ASV: "in [by means of] a
mirror darkly") contains an allusion to mirrors made of polished metal that
at best gave a distorted reflection. "Poor" (ASV: "darkly") is the translation
of the Greek word from which "enigma" comes. It might be literally
rendered "in an enigma" or "enigmatically." The thought is that in this
world we see divine things obscurely, wrapped up as it were in enigmas.
"We do not see the things themselves, but those things as set forth in
symbols and words which imperfectly express them" (Hodge).

The sense of verse 13 is that when the gifts have served their purpose
and ceased to be, there remain "faith [saving faith], hope and love. But
the greatest [cf. 12:31a] of these is love." It is somewhat surprising to see
hope, which speaks of anticipation, in this list. Hodge explains that hope
in one form ceases when it is merged in sight; but in another form it
continues. Some exercises of it "are peculiar to the present state, while
others will never cease. Certain it is that there will always be room even
in heaven . . . for hope of the ever advancing and enlarging blessedness
of the redeemed."

C. The Superiority of Prophecy: The Apostle's Conclusion (14:1–25)

By extolling the excellence of love Paul has prepared his readers to
accept the teaching of the present passage, namely, that "the showy gift of
tongues, on which the Corinthians plumed themselves, is inferior to the
useful gift of prophecy" (Edwards). In the development of the passage
there is first a general affirmation of the superiority of prophecy to the
other gifts (v. 1), then a comparison of tongues and prophecy showing the
latter to be preferable to the former (vv. 2–25).

1. The affirmation of the general superiority of prophecy (14:1)

The first verse is transitional: it briefly alludes to the excellence of love
(set forth in chap. 13) and it introduces the main point of 14:2–25.

The argument of chapters 12 and 13 has shown, among other things, (1)
that the gifts of the Spirit are proper objects of desire, (2) that though they
are all to be valued they are not of equal importance, and (3) that love is of

more worth than any gift. In light of these truths Paul urges his readers: "Follow the way of love and eagerly desire spiritual gifts." In effect, he is saying that "the Corinthians must not infer from the praise so richly heaped on love that the Charismata are of no value; on the contrary, while they ought to pursue the former, let them strive also for excellence in the latter" (Edwards). "Follow the way of" is the translation of a word that literally means to run after, to pursue. It indicates a never-ending action. Findlay understands it to signify prosecuting a thing to its goal. In this context the sense of it is to strive for, seek after, or aspire to. The MLB renders it, "Make love your great guest."

The meaning of "eagerly desire" is not to be sharply distinguished from that of "follow." Both Greek verbs are in the present tense, indicating continuous action. Note how Paul puts the two actions side by side. Williams brings out the sense in translation: "keep on pursuing love, but still keep cultivating your spiritual gifts." Love is not exalted to the disparagement of gifts, but in their interest. It "is not to be pursued by forgetting everything else, but opens the true way to everything else" (Findlay).

"Especially the gift of prophecy" shows that among all the gifts prophecy is to be given the place of priority. The TCNT gives the meaning: "strive for spiritual gifts, above all for the gift of preaching [lit., 'prophecy']."[8]

2. A comparison of tongues and prophecy showing the latter to be superior to the former (14:2–25)

The essence of the passage is that prophecy is to be preferred over tongues—and this for two reasons: (1) It will benefit believers more than tongues will (vv. 2–20) and (2) it will benefit unbelievers more than tongues will (vv. 21–25).

a) Prophecy will benefit believers more than will tongues (14:2–20)

This proposition is first stated (vv. 2–5) and then supported by a number of arguments (vv. 6–20).

1) *The proposition stated* (14:2–5). Three things are asserted in verse 2. First, one who speaks in a tongue does not speak to men, but to God. Second, this means that apart from God, no one hears him understandingly.[9] What he says is just so much sound (cf. 13:1). Third, the reason for

---

[8]Prophecy has some features that correspond to preaching, but the two are not identical.

[9]This is one thing that distinguishes the "tongues" of this passage from the phenomenon of Pentecost (Acts 2), for all those who were present at Jerusalem on the day of Pentecost understood what was being said without benefit of an interpreter.

his not being understood is that "he utters mysteries with his spirit [i.e., not with the mind, the understanding]." Bruce paraphrases to bring out the meaning: "the things that he utters by inspiration are mysteries" (p. 109). "Mystery" in the New Testament denotes a secret (a deep truth of the gospel), its correlative being revelation (not mentioned here). Paul was saying that the tongues-speaker "stops short of disclosure, tantalizing the Church, which hears and hears not" (Findlay).

On the other hand, he who prophesies speaks to men (not to God), and this makes prophecy superior to tongues. At first glance, one might think that a gift used to speak to God is greater than one used to speak to men, but Paul "values gifts for their ability to help men (feeling, no doubt, that God is not as needy)" (Bruner, p. 297). What the prophet speaks is summed up in the words "strengthening" (ASV: "edification," i.e., the building up of Christian character), "encouragement" and "comfort" (v. 3).

The tongues-speaker may benefit himself, but the one who utters prophecy benefits the church (v. 4). "What a difference between one person and the Church!" (Chrysostom, quoted by Robertson and Plummer). Two conclusions are drawn from this statement. First, though Paul would be pleased if all the Corinthians had the gift of tongues, he would prefer that they all prophesy (v. 5a). Second, he who prophesies is greater (i.e., more useful) than he who speaks in tongues, unless he (or someone else, vv. 27–28) interprets for the benefit of the congregation (v. 5b). The interpretation has the practical effect of turning tongues into prophecy and thus puts the glossolalist on a level with the prophet. So, in two acts, he accomplishes what the prophet does in one.

2) *The proposition supported* (14:6–19). Paul's argument in support of his contention that prophecy will benefit believers more than will tongues is in two parts. Verses 6–13 give one series of arguments, verses 14 through 20 give another.

First series of arguments (vv. 6–13). Here we have three levels of argument. In the first Paul, alluding to his approaching visit to Corinth (cf. 4:18ff.; 16:5ff.), makes an appeal to the common sense of the Corinthians (v. 6). What good would it do them if Paul came to them as a mere speaker in tongues, using utterances that were unintelligible to them? Confused mutterings would be of no help to them. Such an approach to their troubled state would be a mockery. Utterance, to be profitable, must be intelligible. "Revelation," "knowledge," "prophecy," and "word of instruction" (v. 6b) tend to shade into one another here, and rigid distinctions should perhaps not be made.

In the second movement the apostle used illustrations, making reference to the sounds of musical instruments (vv. 7–9). What has been said of the uselessness of unintelligible speech sounds is even true of such inanimate instruments as the flute ("pipe," KJV, ASV) and the harp. Robertson and Plummer point out that the flute and the harp were the most common musical instruments in use at banquets, funerals, and religious ceremonies. (They appear to be mentioned here as representative of all wind and string instruments.) Unless the notes they give are distinct, not running confusedly one into the other, no one can tell what is being sounded (v. 7). "The music must be different, if it is to guide people to be joyous, or sorrowful or devout. Soulless instruments can be made to speak a language, but not if all the notes are alike" (Robertson and Plummer). An even stronger example than the flute and the harp is the trumpet (v. 8; "bugle," TCNT, Williams, RSV, et al.). Its sounds are far clearer than theirs, but if it is to be used as a signal its sounds also must be distinct and clear. If they are not, who will prepare for battle? The loudest blast, unless it is unwavering and certain, will be of no use. Indeed, its unintelligible sound could do much harm. "How disastrous, at the critical moment, to doubt whether the trumpet sounds Advance or Retreat!" (Findlay).

Verse 9 applies the illustrations to the matter at hand. "So it is with you. Unless you speak intelligible words with your tongue, how will anyone know what you are saying? You will just be speaking into the air." "Easy to be understood" (ASV) is the translation of a word that means "easily recognizable," "well-marked," "definite," "significant." "Tongue" does not refer to the gift of tongues, but to the organ of speech. Even it, though more expressive than flute or harp or trumpet, may also produce sounds that convey no meaning. "Speaking into the air" is a proverbial expression for ineffectual speech. Weymouth has "talking to the winds."

In the third movement of the argument reference is made to various kinds of languages (lit., "voices," vv. 10–13). Not one of these "fails to convey meaning" (v. 10b, TCNT). Yet even articulate speech is useless to the hearer unless he understands it. There must be a discernible connection between sense and sound. "If then I do not grasp the meaning of what someone is saying, I am a foreigner to the speaker, and he is a foreigner to me" (v. 11).

The application is made in verses 12 and 13: "And so with you; since you are striving for spiritual gifts, be eager to excel in such as will build up the faith of the church. Therefore, let him who, when speaking, uses the gift of 'tongues,' pray for ability to interpret them" (TCNT). The main point is that the readers, in their eagerness for manifestations of the Spirit, should be sure that they are motivated by a desire not for self-gratification, but for the building up of the church. "Spiritual gifts" is the translation of a Greek word that literally means "spirits." It is to be explained in light of 12:7, where it is said that "to each one the manifestation of the Spirit is given." In the present verse it is the different manifestations of the Spirit that are called "spirits" (cf. RSV). Similar are the expressions "spirits of prophets" (14:32), "distinguish between spirits" (12:10), "test the spirits" (1 John 4:1), etc.

From verse 13 the limited value of the gift of tongues may be inferred. The Corinthians were not asked to give it up, but they were encouraged to pray for the added gift of interpretation so that their ecstatic utterances might be of benefit to the church.

Second series of agruments (vv. 14–20). There are three of these. First, the gift of tongues is of relatively less value than other gifts because the faculty of understanding is not involved (vv. 14–15). This is indispensable to meaningful prayer and praise.

One's interpretation of these verses depends in large measure on the meanings given to "spirit" and "understanding." "Spirit" is not a reference to the Holy Spirit. The pronoun "my" is decisive against that view. The most natural way of interpreting the word is to see it as referring to one's own spirit, the person "insofar as he is under the influence of the Spirit of God" (Edwards). The Greek word translated "understanding" means the mind, the intellect, the understanding, the faculty of thinking. Findlay sees it as "the reflective and so-called discursive faculty." For the mind to be "unfruitful" is, according to some interpreters, for it to do no good to others. "There is no [edification] for the congregation, because what [one] utters is not framed by [one's] intellect to convey any meaning to them" (Robertson and Plummer). Barrett says it means one's mind "produces nothing, contributes nothing to the process" (cf. TCNT: "my mind is a blank"). It may mean that the understanding is not benefited, gains no fruit; that is, it does not understand what is said (Chrysostom, Calvin).

Second, the gift of tongues is inferior to other gifts because they are a stumbling block to "the unlearned" (vv. 16–17). To "praise God with your spirit" is to offer thanks to Him. "Those who do not understand" (ASV: "the unlearned") is the translation of a Greek word comes from a word that was used of a private person, an "amateur in contrast to an expert or specialist of any kind" (Arndt and Gingrich; cf. Beck: "an ordinary person"). In Acts 4:13 it is used in the sense of "without special training," "uneducated." In the present passage our first inclination might be to interpret the word as a reference to unbelievers, but verse 23 seems to distinguish those "who do not understand" from unbelievers. Arndt and Gingrich see the word as denoting a kind of catechumen and suggest the word "inquirer" as a definition. Morris, following this, concludes they were "people who had not committed themselves to Christianity, but who were interested." The TCNT renders it "the man . . . who is without your gift." Rotherham and Phillips, similarly, translate it "the ungifted person."

In verse 17 "you" is emphatic, and there may be a touch of irony in the entire statement.

The third argument is drawn from Paul's own experience (vv. 18–19). He, if anyone, had a right to speak with tongues in church, but he would not do it. He makes it clear that he is not putting down a gift that he did not possess: "I thank God that I speak in tongues more than all of you."[10] From this statement it is to be inferred that Paul did not think lightly of the gift of tongues. He thanked God that he excelled in it. However, his fixed conviction on the value of tongues in public worship is clearly reflected in verse 19: "But at a meeting of the Church I would rather speak five words with my mind, and so teach others, than ten thousand words when using the gift of 'tongues'" (TCNT). Williams: "But in the public congregation I would rather speak five words with my mind in action . . . than ten thousand words in ecstasy." "Ten thousand" is the largest number for which the Greeks had a symbol. In light of this it has been suggested that this passage should be rendered, ". . . five words with my mind . . . than an infinite number in a tongue."

Verse 20 may be taken either as a conclusion to the preceding paragraph or as an introduction to what follows: It seems preferable to construe it as a conclusion; in it the apostle appeals to the good sense of his readers. It begins with an affectionate word of address, "Brothers," which softens the sternness of the words that follow: "stop thinking like children." The reference is to the inclination of children to prefer "what glitters and makes a show" over that which is of more value. It is implied that the preference of the Corinthians for showy gifts such as tongues was a mark of childishness. "Thinking," the translation of a word used only in this verse (twice) in the New Testament, means "understanding" (Arndt and Gingrich).

The last half of verse 20 teaches that there is a place for the childlike attitude, but it is in reference to "malice," not thinking (understanding). The paraphrase of Robertson and Plummer expresses the meaning: "Play the part of babies, if you like, in freedom from malice: but in common sense try to act like grownup people."

---

[10]Robertson and Plummer observe that this statement is strong evidence that "tongues are not foreign languages" (p. 314). The apostle does not say that he speaks in more languages (tongues) than the Corinthians, but that he spoke in tongues "more than you all." TCNT: "I use the gift of 'tongues' more than any of you."

c) *Prophecy will benefit unbelievers more than tongues will*
   (14:21–25)

Thus far in this chapter Paul has considered the exercise of spiritual gifts only with reference to their usefulness to the congregation of believers. But apparently unbelievers were sometimes present in the assembly, and it was necessary to avoid giving offense to them. It is with this latter consideration that verses 21–25 have to do. The unit begins with a Scripture quotation (v. 21), and from this draws inferences applicable to the situation at Corinth (vv. 22–25).

The quotation from "the law" (the term is obviously used here for the Old Testament Scriptures generally[11]) is from Isaiah 28:11–12: " 'Through men of strange tongues and through the lips of foreigners I will speak to this people, but even then they will not listen to me,' says the Lord." The prophet was warning Israel that because they mocked at the simple message he had given them from God, as though it were suitable only for children, the Lord would speak to them in another manner. He would deal with them through the lips of the Assyrians, who would conquer them. The "strange" language of this pagan nation would be a judgment of God on Israel, evoking not their faith but confirming and consummating their unbelief.

Commentators struggle to discern the connection of this quotation with the problem at Corinth. It is perhaps as follows: Just as the Israelites who had refused to listen to the clear and intelligible message of Isaiah were punished by being made to listen to speech that was not intelligible, so those who refuse to believe the gospel are punished by hearing "tongues" they cannot understand (cf. Matt. 13:11–12). "God speaks to them unintelligibly only because they are deaf to His clear revelation" (Godet).

Verses 22–25 draw out the implications of Isaiah's prophecy for the Corinthians. Unintelligible "tongues" are a "sign, not for believers, but for the unbelievers" (v. 22a). The context suggests that tongues are for a sign to unbelievers not in the sense that they convince them of their sin but in the sense that they confirm them in their unbelief. Verse 23 gives the clue. It envisions a worship service in which an entire congregation is speaking in tongues. If tongues are (as the Corinthians thought) the highest of the gifts, then to have the whole church using that gift simultaneously would be the supreme manifestation of spiritual power. But the effect would, in fact, be quite different. The assembly "would then resemble nothing so much as a congregation of lunatics!" (Findlay). Those

---

[11]Godet explains that this meaning of the term "law" "is due to the feeling that all the other parts of the Old Testament rest on the law, and themselves form law for believers."

"who do not understand"[12] and the "unbelievers," hearing unintelligible gibberish, will say that the tongues-speakers are mad ("demented," MLB). In this manner they will be confirmed in their unbelief, concluding that this strange phenomenon justifies their negative feelings about Christianity.

The gift of prophecy produces an entirely different effect (vv. 22b–25).[13] If all prophesy (i.e., speak intelligible words under the direct inspiration of God's Spirit) an unbeliever or an unlearned person coming into the assembly will be "convinced [convicted] by all" and "judged by all."[14] The "secrets of his heart" will be "laid bare."[15] He will "fall down and worship God, exclaiming 'God is really among you.'"

D. The Manner of Worship: Practical Directions (14:26–40)

Some interpreters see these verses as setting forth guidelines for the exercise of spiritual gifts; others see them as dealing generally with the conduct of church meetings and as arising from the whole discussion of 11:1–14:25. We agree with the latter but recognize a special bearing of these verses on the matter under discussion in 14:1–25. The passage divides itself quite naturally into four units: the exercise of tongues and prophecy (vv. 26–33a), the role of women (vv. 33b–36), the authority of Paul's instructions (vv. 37,38), and a concluding summary (vv. 39–40).

1. Tongues and prophecy (14:26–33a)

Paul has now answered the question of the relative value of tongues and prophecy. It only remains for him to give practical directions regarding their use.

---

[12]For "those who do not understand" see the comments on 14:16. In the present passage Findlay understands it to mean "uninstructed persons," Robertson and Plummer, "the ungifted or inexperienced Christian." Bruce feels that in verse 16 they were "members of the congregation unversed in glossalalia" but that here (vv. 23 and 24) "they are evidently non-Christians."

[13]There appears to be a discrepancy between verse 22b and verses 24 and 25. In the former, prophecy is said to be for a sign to believers; in the latter it appears to be a sign to unbelievers. Bruce explains that the gift is for a sign to believers "in the sense that it produces believers." Robertson and Plummer say that "the discrepancy is only apparent. The comparison with the disobedient Israelites shows that the [unbelievers] in v. 22 have heard the word and rejected it. [In vv. 24–25] the context shows that the [unbeliever] has not previously heard."

[14]Conybeare: "He is convicted in his conscience by every speaker, he feels himself judged by all."

[15]Conybeare: "The secret depths of his heart are laid open."

The basic principle that must govern the use of all spiritual gifts is given first: "All of these must be done for the strengthening of the church" (v. 26b). "All" is placed first, giving it special emphasis. It is to be inferred from verse 26 that so long as this guideline is observed it is proper for any member of the congregation to contribute to the worship of the church. However, the verse does not mean that it is necessary for every member to have something to contribute to every service.

"What then shall we say, brothers?" may mean "How then stands the case, . . . ?" (Findlay); or "Then what is the right course . . . ?" (Goodspeed). The TCNT renders it, "What do I suggest, then, Brothers?" The NEB has, "To sum up, my friends."

"When you come together" refers to assembling for worship. "Hymn, . . . word of instruction, . . . revelation" suggest the various and typical elements of the worship service. "Hymn" might refer either to an Old Testament Psalm or to an original song.

a) *The exercise of "tongues"* (14:27–28)

The general principle of edification is applied specifically to the exercise of tongues (vv. 27–28) and prophecy (vv. 29–33a), the two gifts that have figured most prominently in Paul's discussion. Four restrictions, all in keeping with the principle of edification, are mentioned with reference to tongues-speaking. First, in a single meeting it is to be "limited to two or three people at the most" (Goodspeed). Second, these are to speak one at a time, that is, in turn. Third, one person is to interpret (v. 27), whether that one person be the speaker or someone else. The use of more than one interpreter could cause delay and/or confusion. Fourth, if there is no one present who is able to interpret, the tongues-speaker is to "keep quiet in the church [assembly]," being content to exercise his gift alone with God (v. 28).

b) *The exercise of prophecy* (14:29–33a)

Three regulations are given for the exercise of the gift of prophecy. First, the number speaking in a single service should be limited to two or three. Others present who possess the prophetic gift are to "weigh what is said" (Goodspeed), "acting as critics of the revelation given through their brethren" (Findlay). The suggestion is that the gifts of prophecy and discerning of spirits (cf. 12:10) were frequently combined (v. 29). Second, if, while another is speaking, a message is revealed to one of these "silent prophets," the speaker is to give way to him (v. 30). It is implied that certain prophets were designated to speak in advance of the service (v. 31). In time, all of them will have opportunity to speak. Third, the prophets, like the tongues-speakers, are to exercise their gift in the service one at a time (v. 31).

Lest any prophet protest that he is irresistibly impelled to speak contrary to the counsel given by Paul there is the reminder that "the spirits [cf. 14:12, where the same Greek word is used] of prophets are subject to the control of prophets" (v. 32). The God who inspires them is not a God "of disorder, but of peace [harmony]" (v. 33a).

2. *The role of women in the church* (14:33b–36)

The instructions set out in these verses are prefaced by the statement that they are in line with *the general custom* of the churches (assemblies) of the saints (i.e., God's people) (v. 33b).[16] It is implied that for women to assume a speaking role in the worship service would have discredited Christianity in the eyes of most people. But Paul does not rest his case on custom alone; he appeals to Scripture (". . . as also the Law says"), probably alluding to Genesis 3:16.

The essence of the passage before us is that women are to "remain silent in the churches [assemblies, congregations]. They are not allowed to speak" (v. 34b). They are to "be in submission ['take a secondary place', MLB]" (v. 34c). They are, in fact, not even to ask questions in the Christian assembly, but are to "ask their own husbands at home."[17] The reason given is that "it is disgraceful for a woman to speak in the church [better, 'in church,' i.e., the assembly]" (v. 35b). What is said here should be compared with 11:2–16, which speaks to the specific question whether Christian women should wear the veil but relates broadly to the relation between man and woman in the Christian order. "Discarding the veil was claiming equality with man; teaching in public was [to exercise authority over man]" (Robertson and Plummer).

There is a seeming contradiction between this ban on the speaking of women in church and the statement of 11:5, which assumes that women "pray" and "prophesy" in the Christian assemblies. The latter verse simply forbids their doing so "with her head uncovered." The matter has been explained variously. For instance, some hold that 11:5 refers to private gatherings, while here it is speaking "in church" that is forbidden. Others think that the present passage has reference to the gift of tongues

---

[16]It is open to debate whether verse 33b concludes the preceding paragraph or introduces the paragraph that follows.

[17]"It is assumed that only married women would think of asking questions in public; unmarried women could get a question asked through the married" (Robertson and Plummer).

and suggest that the words "with tongues" be added after "speak" (v. 35).
Still others feel that Paul is here laying down a general rule and that room
is left for exceptions, such as at Pentecost (where the utterances pro-
ceeded from "all," both men and women [Acts 2:4]) and in the family of
Philip (whose four daughters prophesied [Acts 21:9]). Robertson and
Plummer think it possible that 11:5 is hypothetical. Barrett thinks that
"Paul had been informed of feminist pressure . . . which was contributing seriously to the disorder of the Christian assembly in Corinth, and
took energetic measures to stamp it out. He cannot have disapproved on
principle of contributions made by women to Christian worship and discussion or he would not have allowed xi. 5 to stand in his epistle." Another is then quoted as saying that "Paul is probably alluding in the first
place to a passion for discussion which could give rise to heated argument
between a wife and husband." Calvin adds, in reference to verse 35, that
"it is the part of the prudent reader to consider, that the things of which
[Paul] here treats are intermediate and indifferent, in which there is
nothing unlawful, but what is at variance with propriety and edification."

Verse 36, which is marked by "a tone of indignant protest," implies that
women[18] had been speaking in the Christian congregation at Corinth and
that in permitting this the Corinthian church was striking out on its own,
acting as though they were the Alpha and the Omega of Christian practice. To Paul, they appeared "to be claiming a monstrous amount of
authority and independence" (Robertson and Plummer).

3. The authority of Paul's instructions (14:37–38)

Paul insists that the things he has written to the Corinthians are "the
Lord's command" (v. 37b), and that the best evidence of a man's being a
prophet or being possessed with spiritual gifts will be found in his recognition of this fact. He can prove his own inspiration by acknowledging
Paul's authority.

Verse 38 may be taken in several ways. It may mean that if a man does
not recognize Paul's authority, Paul is through with him; let him remain
in his ignorance. The RSV gives another view: "If any one does not recognize this, he is not recognized." Moffatt reads, "Anyone who disregards
this will be himself disregarded" (at the day of judgment?). Conybeare
puts it similarly: "But if a man refuses this acknowledgement, let him
refuse it at his peril."

---

[18]Not all interpreters agree that verse 36 alludes only to the matter of women speaking in
church. It may take in all the irregularities of the Corinthian church: women discarding the
veil, people getting drunk at the Lord's Supper, the abuse of spiritual gifts, and so forth.

4. A concluding summary (14:39–40)

Three things are brought out. First, prophecy is to be earnestly desired (v. 39a). Second, "tongues" are not to be forbidden (v. 39b). Third, all things must be done decently (with propriety) and in order (in an orderly way) (v. 40).

For Further Study

1. Secure a copy of John R. W. Stott's *The Baptism and Fullness of the Holy Spirit* (InterVarsity) and read it. This is an excellent treatment, and may be read in a short time. Also recommended is Frederick Dale Bruner's *A Theology of the Holy Spirit* (Eerdmans), the subtitle of which is "The Pentecostal Experience and the New Testament Witness." This is a helpful study of the modern charismatic movement in light of the Scriptures.

2. J. W. MacGorman has a useful work on *The Gifts of the Spirit* (Broadman). It is an exposition of 1 Corinthians 12–14.

3. A brief general treatment of the doctrine of the Holy Spirit is Leon Morris's *Spirit of the Living God* (InterVarsity Press). Reference may also be made to Michael Ramsey's *Holy Spirit* (Eerdmans).

4. Make a list of the characteristics of tongues-speaking in Acts 2 and compare this with a similar list drawn up from 1 Corinthians 12–14.

5. Secure a copy of Henry Drummond's famous lecture, *The Greatest Thing in the World*. W. Graham Scroggie has a small book on 1 Corinthians 13 titled *The Love Life* (Kregel).

Chapter 9

The Resurrection of the Dead
(1 Corinthians 15:1–58)

First Corinthians 15 may contain the earliest written account of the Resurrection of Christ, and is the fullest and most important treatment in the Bible of the doctrine of the resurrection of the dead.

Resurrection may be defined as a creative act of God whereby the bodies of dead people are raised to life. It is a distinctly biblical concept, since no form of paganism has any such teaching. Even the Old Testament has few references to resurrection, and these tend to be rather late. This is not surprising, since God's redemptive work in and through the Messiah was progressively revealed. Resurrection hope could come to full flower only after Christ had conquered death and the grave.

Previous sections of the book have treated matters pertaining to church fellowship, morality, idolatry, and worship. Some of these issues had been brought to Paul's attention by members of the household of Chloe; some were perhaps matters of common knowledge among Christians (even those in places far removed from Corinth); others were put to Paul in the form of a letter from the Corinthians. It is not known how the problem concerning the doctrine of the Resurrection was brought to Paul's attention.

Several matters should be kept in mind as one studies this profoundly important passage. One is that the passage speaks of the resurrection of the body, not the immortality of the soul. The two concepts, being quite distinct, should not be thought of as interchangeable. The Greeks found the resurrection of dead bodies inconceivable, and it is not surprising that they ridiculed Paul's proclamation of it in Athens (Acts 17:32). Greek philosophy taught the immortality of the soul; but the body, being matter, was considered evil. Edwards remarks that "no doctrine of Christianity appears to have evoked more stubborn opposition and more contemptuous scorn." Present-day theologians who reject biblical truth as the standard for Christian doctrine tend to reduce resurrection hope to a modern version of the immortality of the soul. That is to say, they reject the doctrine of a bodily resurrection and teach that man's true "self" will continue to exist in an immaterial, ghost-like body made of spirit. The passage before us lends no support to this view. When it speaks of resurrection, it refers to the raising of dead bodies by the power of God.

Again, one should remember that this passage has to do with the resurrection of believers, not of unbelievers. The Scriptures teach that there will be a resurrection of unbelievers (e.g., John 5:28–29), but they give only small attention to that event. First Corinthians 15 is completely silent about it. Paul's concern here is only with the resurrection of those who are in Christ, an event that will take place at His coming.

Finally, it is well to keep in mind that Paul, in writing this chapter, was not fighting a straw man; "some" at Corinth were actually denying the resurrection of the dead (v. 12). But we do not know who these people were, and all the speculative suggestions are unconvincing. Edwards thinks that the word "some" (v. 12) implies that those who denied the Resurrection were relatively few, but of that we cannot be sure.

The chapter falls into two large divisions: verses 1–28, which relate to the Resurrection of Christ; verses 29–58, which speak directly to questions pertaining to the resurrection of believers, those who are "in Christ."

A. The Resurrection of Christ (15:1–28)

The Resurrection of Christ was the coming to life again of the body that was earlier crucified and then placed in lifeless form in the tomb of Joseph. In that very body, transformed indeed and adjusted to its eternal form of existence, Jesus emerged from the tomb never to die again.

To prove that believers will rise from the dead, it was first necessary for Paul to establish the fact that Christ had been raised and to show the interrelatedness of His Resurrection and ours. That is the purpose of the present passage. Its teaching may be summed up under six leading statements.

1. Christ's Resurrection is an essential part of the gospel (15:1–5)

Verses 1 and 2 introduce the matter: "Now, brothers, I want to remind you of the gospel I preached to you, which you received and on which you have taken your stand. By this gospel you are saved, if you hold firmly to the word I preached to you. Otherwise, you have believed in vain." "Remind" is from a word that more exactly means "I make known." It is often used in the New Testament of preaching the gospel. As used in this context, it conveys a tone of gentle rebuke. The idea is that Paul should not have found it necessary to "make known" a message with which the readers had long been acquainted. However, their situation was such that he felt he had to begin again and teach them elementary facts that they had previously accepted.

"Gospel" signifies a joyful announcement, good news, glad tidings. In these verses it is described in four ways: (1) Paul had preached it. The Greek verb for "preached," which literally means to bring or announce good news, is the word of which "evangelize" is a transliteration. (2) The Corinthians had "received" it (i.e. embraced it as true). "Received" was the regular word for receiving a tradition handed down by past teachers. Paul had passed on the gospel to the Corinthians, and he reminds them that they had accepted it in its entirety. (3) On it they had "taken (their) stand." The tense of the verb is perfect, suggesting that they stood firm in their adherence to the gospel. "The immediate implication is that when they denied the resurrection, they denied the very thing in which they stood" (Fisher). (4) By it they are "saved" (cf. 1:18). A present-tense verb, denoting continuous action, is used. It describes the Corinthians' progressive growth in grace. Robertson and Plummer compare "received," "stand," and "saved." Three tenses are used: aorist (simple past), perfect, and present. "Received" looks to the past, "stand" to the present, and "saved" to the future. Paul's readers "accepted his teaching; in it they stand with a firm foothold; and they are thus among . . . those who are in the way of salvation." Findlay observes that the three clauses "describe the inception, continuance, and progressive benefits of the faith of this Church."

Their being saved is conditional on their holding firmly to the word Paul had preached to them. "If you hold firmly" indicates that salvation is conditional on perseverance. The Greek construction shows that Paul was assuming that his readers would "hold firmly." It does not express doubt. "In Paul's thought there is a balance between assurance and presumption. The man who wrote the words found in Romans 5:9–10 could not doubt that his salvation was secure. . . . On the other hand, he recognized the obligation of the Christian to remain a Christian, to be true to his confession of faith . . ." (Fisher). You are saved "if you hold firmly" the gospel. Failure to do this betrays a temporary and therefore inadequate faith.

Verses 3–5 give the essentials of the gospel. They identify these as things that Paul himself had received[1] and which he considered to be of first importance. Four essential elements are named: (1) Christ died (aorist tense, simple historical past) for (i.e. on account of, in order to deal

---

[1]The point is that Paul did not invent this gospel; it did not originate with him.

with) our sins according to the Scriptures. The latter words suggest that
the death of Christ was in the purpose of God. (2) He was buried (evidence that Christ's death was real). (3) He has been raised (perfect tense,
suggesting that He was raised and continues to live). The Resurrection is
said to have occurred on the third day and to be in accordance with
prophetic Scriptures. (4) He appeared to witnesses.[2]

2. Christ's Resurrection was historically attested by many witnesses (15:5–10)

The list of witnesses begins with Peter, the first of the apostles to see
the risen Lord, and ends with Paul, the "least" and last of the apostles.
The list is only representative, not exhaustive, and is intended to show
how well founded is belief in the Resurrection. In addition to Peter and
Paul the list includes "the Twelve,"[3] the "more than five hundred" to
whom the Lord appeared at one time, "James" (the Lord's brother?), "all
the apostles" (obviously excluding Judas).[4]

Paul's vision on the Damascus Road, coming "last of all," is put on the
same level as the other appearances. It was, he says, "as to one abnor-
mally born" (v. 8). Possibly this unusual description of himself is intended
to point to his violent and unnatural entrance into the circle of believers.
Arndt and Gingrich suggest that the Greek word, which literally means
"miscarriage," was a term of contempt that perhaps Paul's enemies had
hurled at him (cf. Moffatt: "this so-called abortion of an apostle"). The
figure may, on the other hand, simply reflect Paul's sense of unworthi-
ness. "It indicates his intense feeling respecting the errors of his career
previous to his conversion" (Robertson and Plummer). Verses 9 and 10, a
somewhat parenthetical statement expressing Paul's deep humility, lend
support to this view.

3. Christ's Resurrection was uniformly preached by all the apostles and was believed by the Corinthians (15:11)

"Whether, then, it was I or whether it was they [the other apostles, cf.
vv. 9–10], this we proclaim, and this you believed (when we preached to

---

[2]Verse 5 connects both with what precedes it and with that which follows it.

[3]"The Twelve" had apparently become a sort of official name for the group, hence the use
of the number "twelve," even though Judas was no longer among them. If the reference is to
the appearance on the evening of the first Lord's day, Thomas was absent also.

[4]The reference could be to the appearance recorded in John 20:26ff. or to that given in
Acts 1:1ff.

you)" (TCNT). "The resurrection of Christ," writes Hodge, "was included in the preaching of all ministers, and in the faith of all Christians." One may, if he so chooses, deny that the Resurrection of Christ occurred, but if he does he contradicts all apostolic teaching and leaves himself without a gospel.

4. Christ's Resurrection is fundamental to salvation and all else that relates to Christian experience (15:12–19)

It is "not an isolated fact or doctrine which can be accepted or rejected independently of other truths" (Robertson and Plummer). The following points are made: The apostle shows first that to deny the possibility of the resurrection of believers leads logically to the denial of the Resurrection of Christ; the grounds on which the one is excluded make the other also impossible (vv. 12–13). Paul's argument is that "the absolute philosophical denial of bodily resurrection precludes the raising up of Jesus Christ" (Findlay).

Next, the apostle shows how unspeakably tragic the situation is if Christ has not been raised (vv. 14–19). Five consequences are enumerated: (1) If Christ has not been raised, the whole gospel is subverted; "our preaching" (the testimony of Paul and his fellow apostles; cf. v. 11) "is useless" and "so is your faith" (v. 14). "More than that" is in verse 15. My comment is about a word used by the ASV in verse 14. The NIV does not translate the Greek which lies behind this word. It would, in light of this, be best to omit the sentence beginning with "More than that." "Preaching" means what is preached, the substance of preaching rather than the act. "Useless," placed first in both of the Greek clauses, means hollow, empty, meaningless, "void of all truth, reality, and power" (Hodge). If the Resurrection is not actual and real, then both the apostolic message and the faith it elicits are without meaning.

(2) If Christ has not been raised, the apostles "are found to be false witnesses about God" (v. 15). That is, they are found (discovered, detected) to be men who lie about God, affirming that He did something that He in fact did not do. Either Christ rose from the dead or the apostles lied in affirming that He did. The apostle's "evident horror of being convicted at the bar of Divine justice of bearing false witness in this matter shows his estimate of the importance of the matter" (Robertson and Plummer).

(3) If Christ has not been raised, "your faith is futile; you are still in your sins" (v. 17). The word for "futile" is different from that for "useless," found in verse 14. There it is *kenos*, meaning empty, without substance, lacking reality. Here it is *mataia*, meaning fruitless, ineffectual, lacking in results. In verse 3 it has been affirmed that "Christ died

for our sins," but if He was not raised from the dead His death has no redemptive power and we are left in our sins. Hodge appropriately comments, "Many allow themselves to entertain doubts as to this very doctrine of the resurrection of the body, who would be shocked at the thought of rejecting the doctrine of atonement. Yet Paul teaches that the denial of the one involves the denial of the other."

(4) If Christ has not been raised (making faith ineffectual and leaving believers in their sins), then those who "have fallen asleep in Christ are lost" (v. 18). "Fallen asleep" is a euphemism for death. To fall asleep "in Christ" is to die believing in Him. "Are lost," which is an aorist tense, might be translated by the simple past tense ("perished"). The thought is, they perished when they died. "If Christ did not rise for the justification of those who died in Him, they found no advocate at the bar of God; and have incurred the fate of those who perish in their sins" (Hodge). Perishing (being "lost") does not mean annihilation; it "denotes a state of perdition in which the soul remains under the weight of Divine condemnation" (Godet).

(5) If Christ has not been raised from the dead, not only did the departed sink into eternal ruin when they died, but we who are alive and have put "hope in Christ" "are to be pitied more than all men" (v. 19). The thought of the verse is that if hope in Christ is limited to this life, then Christians are a people above all others to be pitied. They have renounced this world for the world to come, only to discover in the end that there is no world to come.

5. Christ's Resurrection is the pledge and pattern of the believer's resurrection (15:20–23)

This thought is stated in verse 20, explained in verses 21 and 22, and qualified in verse 23.

The statement of the fact is found in verse 20. "But Christ has indeed been raised from the dead, the firstfruits of those who have fallen asleep." "But" (ASV: "But now") marks the point that the argument has reached. Its force is: "As the matter now stands." "Has indeed been raised from the dead" gathers up the central thought of the preceding verses and boldly affirms its truth as an established fact. In describing Christ as "the firstfruits of those who have fallen asleep" Paul shows that He has been raised in a representative character. The word "firstfruits" suggests three things: First, Christ was the first to rise from the dead.[5] Second, His Resurrection is a guarantee of the resurrection of all who are in Him. As

---

[5]Others, such as Lazarus, the daughter of Jairus, etc., had been brought from death to life, but it is assumed that they died again. Christ was the first to rise never to die again.

Hodge explains, "The apostle does not mean merely that the resurrection of Christ was to precede that of his people; but as the first sheaf of the harvest presented to God as a thank-offering was the pledge and assurance of the ingathering of the whole harvest, so the resurrection of Christ is a pledge and proof of the resurrection of his people." The earth is eventually to yield a great harvest of glorified bodies, and Christ is the firstfruit of that harvest. His people's resurrection is assured by His; His Resurrection is the first installment, a pledge that many more are to come. Third, as the first sheaf offered to God was the same in kind as the rest of the harvest, so Christ's Resurrection is the pattern of His people's.

The fact is explained in verses 21 and 22. Verse 21 shows that just as there is a causal relation between the death of Adam and the death of his descendants, so there is a causal relation between the Resurrection of Christ and the resurrection of His people. "In different ways, Adam and Christ were each of them Head of the human race and could represent it" (Robertson and Plummer). We die by virtue of our union with Adam; we live by virtue of our union with Christ.[6]

This is qualified in verse 23. Christ's Resurrection secures that of His people, but the two events do not occur at the same time. There is a proper order for each. The word for "turn" (Gr., *tagma*), originally a military term for a detachment or company of soldiers, is used here to suggest simply that those experiencing resurrection are in two divisions— one made up of the solitary figure of Christ, the other composed of those who belong to Him (His people). He, as firstfruit, is raised first; they are to be raised "when he comes" (lit., "at his coming"). The latter word, in ancient times a technical term used for the arrival of a king or his representative, refers to Christ's second advent at the end of the age.

6. *Christ's Resurrection is the first state in His complete triumph over evil* (15:24–28)

Death is the last enemy to be destroyed, but the process of destruction was begun with the Resurrection of Christ. With His Resurrection the decisive battle was won and ultimate victory was assured. All that remains is the "mopping up" work. At the coming of Christ His people will be raised, all opposition to the rule of God will be abolished, and the kingdom will be delivered up to the Father.

---

[6]Verse 22 can be understood in either of two ways: (1) Just as all who are in Adam (the entire race) die, even so all who are in Christ (believers) shall be made alive. (2) Just as all believers by virtue of their union with Adam die, even so all believers by virtue of their union with Christ shall be made alive.

"Then the end will come" is a reference to the termination of world history. It is debated whether there is an interval between Christ's coming and the end. Robertson and Plummer conclude that it is not possible to say, for the Greek word for "then" "may introduce either what is subsequent or what is immediately consequent." Those who argue for an interval ordinarily see this sequence in the resurrection of the dead: (1) Christ, "the firstfruits," (2) believers in Christ "when he comes," and (3) all the rest of mankind at "the end," when the final judgment takes place. These interpreters commonly interpose the millennium between (2) and (3). It must be admitted that the text is not decisive on this matter. Hodge, who argues against an interval, says the text "marks the succession of certain events, but determines nothing as to the interval between them." He adds, however, that "the natural impression is that nothing remains to be done after the resurrection before the end comes." In other words, the coming is the end. Bruce thinks the context suggests that the interval is short. Fisher interprets "end" to mean "goal." "The implication is that God has a goal toward which he is working in history. The decisive event in history was the Christ event, but the climactic event in which that event finds its consummation is the perfect rule of God."

"The end" (or goal) is defined as the time (or event) "when he [Christ] delivers the kingdom to God the Father after destroying every [hostile] rule and every [hostile] authority and power" (RSV). "Destroying" is the translation of a Greek word that essentially means "to put out of work," "make inoperative," "render null and void."

Christ's conquest over evil is consummated in the resurrection of the dead. "The last enemy to be destroyed [made inoperative] is death" (v. 26). Verse 27a provides Scripture proof for the assertion that death shall be abolished. The passage cited is Psalm 8, where the subjection of all things to the Messiah is predicted. "For he [the Father] has put everything under his [the Messiah's] feet." Verse 27b shows that "everything" obviously does not include God the Father, who put everything under His Son.

When Christ has fully accomplished His mediatorial mission, He will place Himself under the Father, that God may be all in all (v. 28). For God to be "all in all" is for Him to have unchallenged supremacy.

Bruce points out that "the kingdom of Christ comes to an end in its present phase, but only to merge in the eternal kingdom of God." Hodge explains that this verse is to be seen as parallel with the statement of verse 24. "The subjection of the Son to the Father here means precisely what is there meant by his delivering up the kingdom of God . . . . The thing done, and the person who does it, are the same." Findlay comments that "this implies no inferiority of nature, no extrusion from power, but the free submission of love . . . , which is the essence of the filial spirit that actuated Christ from first to last." Christ is not inferior to the Father in His person, but He is subordinate in His function as Mediator/Messiah.

B. The Resurrection of Believers (15:29–58)

Having established the truth of Christ's Resurrection and having shown that the resurrection of His people is assured by that event, Paul is ready now to deal more directly with various questions relating to a future bodily resurrection. There are three principal divisions: (1) the practical importance of the Resurrection (vv. 29–34), (2) the nature of the resurrection body (vv. 35–49), and (3) a concluding summary (vv. 50–58).

1. Practical importance of the Resurrection (15:29–34)

The matter is approached from a negative perspective: "What will those do . . . ? If the dead are not raised at all . . . . If the dead are not raised . . ." (vv. 29, 32). "What" (v. 29a; ASV: "else") translates a word that means "otherwise"; the idea is, "assuming that there is no Resurrection." Three practical conclusions are drawn: First, if the dead are not raised, it is absurd to embrace Christianity (v. 29). The crux of this most difficult verse is found in the phrase "baptized for the dead." More than thirty interpretations have been proposed; therefore, humility, charity, and openness are especially important in approaching this text. No interpretation is without its problems, but the one that has most to commend it understands the passage as referring to persons who, bereaved of loved ones who were believers, turned to Christ in the hope of a blessed reunion—as in the case of a son led to Christ by his dying mother's appeal, "Meet me in heaven!" If there is no resurrection, argues Paul, such an act has no meaning at all. But if resurrection is real and faith is real, the expectation of such a reunion will not prove to be a delusion.

In this interpretation, "the dead" (observe the article, denoting a particular class of the dead) are the dead in Christ; baptism is true Christian baptism (not vicarious baptism), such as Paul could approve; the pronoun "those" refers to those who, moved by the faith and love of those who died in the Lord, embraced Christ; and "for" (Gr., *hyper*) means "with reference to."[7] The positive teaching of this verse is that *belief in the Resurrection imparts hope.*

---

[7]Many interpreters prefer to see in this verse a reference to vicarious baptism. They explain that this was being practiced at Corinth (perhaps by a minority in the church) but point out that Paul did not approve of the practice. This interpretation is clearly stated in Morris's commentary. Parry says any other interpretation is an evasion.

Second, if the dead are not raised, it makes no sense to expose one's self to danger in propagating Christianity (vv. 30–32a). Paul uses his own experience to make this point. "And I too, why do I put my life to hazard every hour?" (v. 30, Conybeare). Verse 31, equivalent to an oath, is a strong affirmation of the apostle's constant peril. Verse 32a is a specific instance of the same. The positive teaching of these verses is that *belief in the Resurrection inspires sacrificial service.*

Third, if there is no resurrection, it is folly to insist on moral standards (v. 32b). As Barrett puts it, "If death is the end, there is little left to do but pluck the pleasure of the passing moment." The positive teaching of this verse is that *belief in the Resurrection is a strong motive to high morals* (cf. 1 John 3:3).

The unit closes with a solemn warning against associating with those (e.g., the pagans of Corinth) who doubt such fundamentals of the faith as the Resurrection (v. 33) and an urgent appeal to the readers to rouse themselves from their moral stupor (v. 34).

2. *Nature of the resurrection body* (15:35–49)

Paul has set forth the Resurrection of Christ as the grounds for belief in the resurrection of the Christian. He has also shown the disastrous consequences of rejecting the hope of resurrection. Now he turns to consider the question of the nature of the resurrection body.

Two questions open the discussion: "But someone may ask, 'How are the dead raised? With what kind of body will they come?'" (v. 35). The "someone" is probably an imagined opponent of the principle of resurrection. The first question intimates that resurrection is impossible; the second that it is inconceivable. The second question expands on and attempts to justify the first. Findlay paraphrases it: "In what bodily form do we picture the dead coming on the scene?" Paul's answer is in four parts.

First, he illustrates from nature *the possibility of a resurrection body* (vv. 36–38). The mystery of the Resurrection should raise no question of the possibility of the Resurrection, for "the same mystery is wrapped up in every germinating seed" (Findlay). A person totally ignorant of farming, watching the farmer plant seed in the spring, might ask, "What sort of body can come from a dry grain that you drop into the earth to rot?" But the sower, having witnessed the process of quickening so frequently, would dismiss the questioner as a fool. Paul was arguing that the actuality of this lower type of "resurrection" vindicates the conceivability of the higher.

A few matters deserve comment. For instance, the pronoun "you" (v.

36), emphatic in the Greek, reminds the readers that Paul is referring to something familiar to them. Again, the verb translated "come to life" (v. 36; ASV "is . . . quickened") is passive, implying that the seed does not germinate and grow of itself but that it is acted on by an outside agent. That agent, the context suggests, is God. It is implied that the God who can quicken the lifeless seed can also quicken our mortal bodies. To deny this is to impugn the power and resources of the Creator. Moreover, the seed that is sown is different from that which grows out of it; "you do not plant the body that will be" (v. 37). From this it is to be inferred that the resurrection body, though having some sort of continuity with the present body, will be different from it. Finally, verse 38 sums up the principal teaching of this section: the resurrection body will be the body God is pleased to give us; just as He gives to each seed (think of it!) a body of its own, He will give to each believing person a body suitable for his or her redeemed self.

Second, Paul shows that God is capable of producing *various kinds of bodies* (vv. 39–41). There is in fact an amazing variety of bodies in God's creation, and there is a fitness of each for that which it clothes. Why then should anyone think that there can be only one kind of human body, and that that body is the one known to this life? God can give us the kind of body we need.

Third, Paul teaches that the resurrected body will be *gloriously different* from the present body (vv. 42–46). Just as heavenly bodies (planets? angelic beings?) differ from earthly bodies, and as one star differs from another star, so the resurrection body will differ from the present earthly body. Paul's purpose in making this statement was to show how groundless is the objection to the Resurrection that assumes that the resurrection body must be like the body of flesh and blood. Verses 42b–44 indicate, by means of a series of antitheses, some of the differences between the present body and the body that is to be.

This present body that is "sown [continuing the imagery of seed][8] is perishable"; that is to say, it is sown a perishable body, a body subject to disease, death, and decay. The body that is sown will be "raised imperishable." That is, the resurrection body will be a body no longer subject to dissolution and decay (v. 42b). The present body is sown "in dishonor," lacking in attractiveness. The word suggests disability, perhaps disfigurement. Goodspeed renders it "humiliation." The primary reference is to

---

[8]Several commentators think the "sowing" need not be burial; "this mortal life may itself be the sowing that is followed by the harvest of resurrection life" (Bruce).

the body at the time of death and burial. At the end of this age it will be "raised in glory." The basic meaning of "glory" is "splendor"; hence, it is interpreted by Hodge as "that resplendent brightness which diffuses light and awakens admiration" (cf. Phil. 3:21). In the present passage the idea may be "beauty" (v. 43a; cf. TCNT). Again, the body is "sown in weakness; it is raised in power" (v. 43b). Weakness marks the earthly body even in life; the primary reference here, however, is to the corpse. The weakness that belongs to the body in life "is perfected in death." "Nothing is more absolutely powerless than a corpse—it can do nothing and it can resist nothing" (Hodge). In this context, "power" suggests that the resurrection body will possess faculties of which we now have no conception.

The final couplet, which serves to gather up all that has been said in this series of antitheses, affirms that what is sown is "a natural body" and what is raised is "a spiritual body" (v. 44a). "Natural" comes from *psychikon*, "pertaining to the soul." Arndt and Gingrich explain that the term always denotes "the life of the natural world and whatever belongs to it, in contrast to the supernatural world." A "natural" body is a body adapted to and expressive of the *psyche*, the rational principle of life. Goodspeed renders it "physical body." Mrs. Montgomery has, "The body sown is animal." The term essentially points up that the body we now have is suited to our present, earthly existence. A "spiritual body" is a body suited to a higher level of life; it is a body that expresses spirit and is adapted to a supernatural, spiritual environment.

In the last part of verse 44, Paul justifies his assertion about a "spiritual body," an expression that at first may appear to be a contradiction in terms, almost the same as "immaterial matter." In effect he says, if it is proper to speak of a "natural" body (i.e., a body suited to the *psyche*), it is also proper to speak of a "spiritual" body (i.e., a body suited to the needs of the spirit). If the one exists, the other does also. The TCNT says: "As surely as there is a human body, there is also a spiritual body."

Verse 45 shows that what has been said about "natural" and "spiritual" bodies is in keeping with the teachings of the Scriptures. Picking up the ideas of "natural" (*psychikos*, pertaining to the soul) and "spiritual" (*pneumatikos*, pertaining to the spirit), Paul quotes a passage that represents Adam as having been created a "living soul"; he became a *psyche* and had a body adapted to it. He was created for an existence on this earth and was given a body suitable for such existence. The last Adam (Christ) became "a life-giving spirit." Christ is the "last Adam" because He is the second representative Man, of whom Adam is said elsewhere to be the type or pattern (Rom. 5:14). Adam was, however, a creature possessing animal life and belonging to the natural order. Christ, on the other hand, though by His incarnation one of us, belongs to a higher order, is linked to the supernatural, the world of spirit. He has life in Himself, and can give that life to as many as He wishes (cf. John 5:21, 26).

Verse 46 does not simply teach that the natural body precedes the spiritual. Rather, it states a general principle: the natural (the lower, the imperfect) precedes the spiritual (the higher, the perfect). Our present, earthly state is preparatory to the eternal state. "The present life is like a seed time, the harvest is hereafter" (Hodge).

Fourth, Paul concludes that *the resurrection body will be a body like Christ's* (vv. 47–49). The heart of these verses is found in the statement of verse 49: "And just as we have borne the likeness of the earthly man, so shall we bear the likeness of the man from heaven." The promise contained in these words holds true, of course, only for those who have a vital union with Christ. But for them, the wearing of "His moral likeness here carries with it the wearing of His bodily likeness hereafter" (Findlay).

3. *A concluding summary* (15:50–58)

Paul comes now to the conclusion of his discussion of the resurrection of the dead. The entire paragraph is like a paean of victory. In it the apostle brings together several strands of thought that have appeared earlier. All of it may be summed up under three leading statements:

a) *The Resurrection is a necessity for the life to come* (15:50–53)

In developing this idea Paul first asserts that "flesh and blood cannot inherit the kingdom of God, nor does the perishable inherit the imperishable" (v. 50). Though the statement is made negatively, it implies the positive thought that some sort of change in the physical body is necessary if it is to share in the eternal age. Godet writes that the formula "I declare to you" (v. 50a) is used by Paul to "announce a decisive and final explanation . . . which will put the truth previously stated in its full light." However, the force of it may be simply "What I mean is this."

"Flesh and blood" is a description of the present earthly body; the wording may perhaps suggest its frailty. Barrett thinks the phrase is simply Paul's way of referring to living persons: "Living men cannot inherit God's kingdom." "Inherit" is not to be pressed literally. Its general sense is "to possess," have a share in. "Perishable" is understood by some to be an abstract term referring to "flesh and blood." Its clause is then taken to be a restatement in more general language of the thought of verse 50a (cf. Findlay). Barrett thinks the term is a reference to the bodies of those who have died. In other words, the first line of verse 50 "refers to those who are alive at the parousia, the second line to those who died before the parousia."

Verse 50 has indicated the incompatibility of the physical body with the eternal order. This implies that *all* believers must therefore be given new bodies—the dead through resurrection, and the living (i.e., those living at the return of Christ) through change. Verses 51 and 52 announce on the authority of a momentous revelation from God how these new bodies will be provided.

"Listen" (v. 51) arrests attention. "I tell you a mystery" is an "emphatic introduction of information of great moment" (Robertson and Plummer). "Mystery" (secret) denotes a divine truth undiscoverable apart from divine revelation. The word is generally used by Paul of a truth not known (fully) by previous generations but is now made clear in the gospel. Every time Paul uses it he combines it with some word that suggests revelation, manifestation, making known, etc. The mystery essentially concerns the transformation of those who will be alive when Christ returns. The following truths are contained in it: First, not all Christians will "sleep" (die). Those who are living when Christ returns will be spared this experience (cf. 1 Thess. 4:15). Second, all Christians will be changed. Third, this change will occur "in a flash, in the twinkling of an eye, at the last trumpet." The first two phrases describe the instantaneousness of the transformation, the last its solemn finality. "Moment" is the translation of *atomos*, a term meaning "that which cannot be cut." It was used by the ancients of an indivisible unit of time. (Our word "atom" comes from it.) "Twinkling" suggests the time it takes for the casting of a glance or the fluttering of an eyelid. The trumpet call is described as the "last" because it will be the last ever to sound, not because it is the last in a series. The entire phrase suggests that the events described—transformation of the bodies of the living and resurrection of the bodies of the dead—will occur on the last day of the age (cf. Matt. 24:31). Fourth, the change in the bodies of the living will occur in connection with the resurrection of the dead, the sequence perhaps being resurrection of the dead then the change of the living (note the order of the statements in v. 52b; cf. 1 Thess. 4:16,17).

The necessity for the transformation of our bodies, stated in a negative way in verse 50, is affirmed positively in verse 53: "For the perishable must clothe itself with the imperishable, and the mortal with immortality." The TCNT: "For this perishable body of ours must put on an imperishable form, and this dying body a deathless form." "This perishable" and "this mortal" are to be taken as synonymous, both phrases referring to the present, living body. "Must" is the translation of a word that denotes a compulsion of any kind—of divine destiny, of duty, of law, of inner necessity, etc. Here it is used of the compulsion of what is fitting. "To clothe" represents the change as an investiture with incorruption and immortality. The metaphor "implies that there is a permanent element continuing under the new conditions" (Robertson and Plummer).

b) The Resurrection is the defeat of death (15:54–57)

For now, death seems to triumph; it does conquer and destroy; but its conquest is only temporary. "When the perishable has been clothed with the imperishable, and the mortal with immortality, then [and only then] the saying that is written will come true: "Death has been swallowed up in victory" (v. 54). The "saying" is a quotation of Isaiah 25:8. Findlay (quoting Dillmann) calls this "the farthest reaching of all O. T. prophecies; it bears allusion to Gen. iii . . . , and reverses the doom there pronounced." The "swallowing up" of death suggests that the victory of Christ and His people will be complete and final. Goodspeed renders it, "Death has been triumphantly destroyed."

In verse 55 Paul, adapting the words of Hosea 13:14, seems to taunt and challenge death. His words form a shout of triumph. John Donne's eloquent lines are apropos:

> Death, be not proud, though some have called thee
> Mighty and dreadful, for thou art not so:
> For those whom thou think'st thou dost overthrow
> Die not, poor Death; nor yet canst thou kill me.
>
> . . . . Why swell'st thou then?
> One short sleep past, we wake eternally,
> And Death shall be no more: Death, thou shalt die!

In speaking of the "sting" of death the apostle depicts death as a venomous serpent inflicting fatal wounds. Christ, however, has drawn its sting and left it powerless. In saying that the sting of death "is sin" (v. 56a) Paul means that sin gives to death its penal character and makes it a fearful thing: "It is not *death* in itself that is the harmful thing. It is *death* that is 'the wages of sin' (Rom. vi. 23) that matters. . . . The *sting* is not in *death*, but in *sin*" (Morris, p. 235). In saying that "the power of sin is the law" (v. 56b) Paul alludes to the fact that the law in some sense stimulates sin and gives it its character of rebellion.

Verse 57, which should be compared to Romans 7:25, has been described as an "exclamation of relief": "but thanks be to God! He gives us the victory through our Lord Jesus Christ." "He gives" is the translation of a present tense participle, suggesting that although full victory is yet to come, the process that leads to it is already going on. The "victory" for which Paul gives thanks is the victory over death. That victory comes through Jesus Christ, who has satisfied all the demands of the law, made propitiation for our sins, and conquered the grave—thus destroying the strength of sin and removing the sting from death.

c) *The Resurrection is an incentive to service* (15:58)

The chapter closes with an exhortation. "Therefore, my dear brothers, stand firm, unshaken, always diligent in the Lord's work, for you know that, in union with him, your toil is not in vain" (TCNT). "Therefore" indicates that the appeal of this verse is drawn as an inference from the preceding discussion of the defeat of death. The exhortation is twofold: (1) to have a stable, fixed, unshakeable purpose—especially concerning the truth of the Resurrection; and (2) to abound in the work of the Lord, that is, apply themselves fully to it. As an encouragement to the doing of these things, Paul reminds the Corinthians that their labor is not empty and meaningless in the Lord, as would be true if there were no resurrection.

For Further Study

1. Study the records of the Resurrection of Jesus in the Gospels and compare the appearances listed there with those in 1 Corinthians 15. Make a comprehensive list of all the appearances.

2. Secure a copy of Frank Morrison's *Who Moved the Stone?* (Zondervan), and read it. The author, an English journalist, set out to prove that the story of Christ's Resurrection was myth. But through his studies he came to be a believer in the risen Christ.

3. Helpful articles on the Resurrection may be found in Bible encyclopedias and dictionaries, such as *The Zondervan Pictorial Encyclopedia of the Bible*.

4. Compare Romans 5:12ff. with the statement about Adam and Christ in 1 Corinthians 15:21 and 22.

5. Read the addresses of Acts, making note of all references to the resurrection of Christ.

6. Use a hymn book to study hymns about the resurrection of Christ.

Chapter 10

The Collection for the Saints
(1 Corinthians 16:1–9)

Paul has completed his discussion of theological themes in 1 Corinthians, and he now turns to practical matters. The collection for Jerusalem mentioned in this passage was an enterprise highly valued by Paul. During an earlier visit of Paul and Barnabas to Jerusalem an agreement had been reached with leaders concerning their respective spheres of ministry (Gal. 2:1–10). At this time the leaders of Jerusalem had asked Paul to remember the poor among the Jerusalem church, and Paul indicated his eagerness to do this (Gal. 2:10). During his ministry in the Aegean Sea area he led the gentile churches that he had planted to contribute funds for the needy at Jerusalem, and the reference in 1 Corinthians is the first mention in writing concerning this collection. Later Paul discusses the project in 2 Corinthians 8 and 9 and in Romans 15:25–28. The contribution of these gentile churches served at least three purposes: (1) an acknowledgment by gentile churches of the spiritual debt owed to the Jerusalem church; (2) an obvious demonstration of the genuineness of faith of the gentile Christians; (3) a method of linking Jewish and gentile Christians more closely together (Bruce).

Paul's directions in this section are thorough and sound. They demonstrate that the great saint and theologian was an excellent administrator. His directions cover the time and manner of personal contributions. They also concern the method of transporting funds from Corinth to Jerusalem. His final words of this section prepare the Corinthians for a coming visit.

A. The Time and Method of Contribution (16:1–2)

The phrase, "Now about," in verse 1 may suggest that the Corinthians had asked Paul about this matter of collecting money, and Paul may have been answering their inquiry (cf. 7:1). The saints mentioned here are those of the Jerusalem church. There is no written record of Paul's instructions to the Galatian churches, but Paul likely mentioned their names to indicate to the Corinthians that they were not the only Gentiles asked to support Jewish Christians.

Greek brotherhoods often helped pagan Greeks. Jews often helped poor Jews. It would have been shameful if Christians were to fall behind Jews and pagans in caring for the poor. Some have suggested that the particular financial need among Jerusalem Christians may have been caused by the community of goods that prevailed for a time (Acts 4:32–37). Godet feels that unbelieving Jews must have made economic paupers of Jewish Christians and reduced them to a state of abject dependence from which churches in gentile territories would be free.

Paul's use of "the first day" in verse 2 suggests that Sunday had become the day when Christians were meeting for worship (Acts 20:7; Rev. 1:10). The phrase "set aside" suggested that the money was to be left at home, not brought to the church treasurer. These successive deposits, even if quite small, would eventually become a store or a treasure. The giving was to be proportional, in direct response to the way in which the person was prospering financially. This receiving of funds was to be accomplished by the time of Paul's arrival so that he would not need to beg. His recommended method would avoid a final scramble for funds and underline individual responsibility over a period of time. It was a sound administrative technique.

B. The Method of Distribution (16:3–4)

Paul's plans for arrival were still uncertain, but his plans for handling the distribution of funds were fixed and sensible. He intends neither to handle the money nor to appoint their representatives for carrying it to Jerusalem. He wisely protects his own position and integrity. If he does not go, he will provide the envoys with letters of recommendation that will commend them to the leaders of the church in Jerusalem. The word "approve" suggests that the Corinthians must select those who were worthy and morally proven for this task. No potential spiritual dropout should be a candidate.

Some have suggested that the "if" of verse 4 is inserted to indicate that if the sum of money is large enough, Paul intends to accompany the envoys to Jerusalem (Morris). It may be more likely that Paul indicates that the circumstances of God's will both in Jerusalem and elsewhere will suggest the advisability of his accompanying the delegates. He eventually decided to go to Jerusalem (Rom. 15:25) and later arrived with these funds (Acts 20:16; 21:17; 24:17).

Paul's sensible suggestions for handling these funds would protect his integrity at a time when accusations against religious charlatans were common. Christian leaders today must not exhibit naiveté in financial matters but must wisely serve as examples of economic accountability. To do otherwise will allow the enemies of the Lord to blaspheme the people of God and the practice of Christianity.

C. Paul's Plans for a Visit (16:5–9)

Paul states in verse 5 his plan for visiting Corinth. It is similar to a plan indicated in Acts 19:21 and suggested that Paul would come to Corinth after first having passed through Macedonia. The use of the present tense for the latter verb, "go through," suggests that his intention to follow these plans is firm. However, circumstances did modify his plans, and he made an unexpected visit to Corinth not mentioned in Acts but suggested in 2 Corinthians 2:1 by his reference to a "painful visit." This visit was made necessary by an outbreak of spiritual opposition to Paul in Corinth and occurred after the writing of 1 Corinthians.

Paul intended to winter in Corinth whenever he did arrive (v. 6). Travel by sea in the Mediterranean area was considered dangerous during the autumn season and was entirely suspended during the winter months. Paul seems to have spent a winter at Corinth before setting out for Jerusalem (Acts 20:2; Rom. 16:23). He desired that the Corinthians send him on his way by their good wishes and prayers. Bruce suggests that Paul did not visit Corinth during the next winter after writing 1 Corinthians, but it was the winter following that.

Paul's plans at this time were still flexible, but he wanted to convey to the Corinthians a desire to linger with them (v. 7). He did not desire to make a passing, brief visit, for this would be unsatisfying. However, since he is the Lord's servant, any firm plan is subject to His direction.

Paul's immediate task is at Ephesus, and he will not be finished with his responsibility there until Pentecost (v. 8). Pentecost, the Feast of Weeks, was the festival of wheat harvest that took place seven weeks after the presentation of first fruits (Lev. 23:15–21). Since this was a spring festival, it is likely that Paul was writing 1 Corinthians during the spring. Paul's reference to Pentecost does not suggest that Christian churches were celebrating a Christian Pentecost at this early date but rather that Paul was planning his journeys by the Jewish sacred year.

In verse 9 Paul indicated that a significant door of opportunity had opened at Ephesus, but there was also a frightening amount of opposition. Both facts suggested reasons why Paul should not immediately leave Ephesus. Some of Paul's opposition in Ephesus is indicated by the outbreak in Acts 19. Williams renders verse 9: "For I have an opportunity here that is great and calls for work, and it has many opponents." Paul's indomitable spirit would not be intimidated by intense opposition and great personal risk.

It is instructive to compare Paul's words in 16:5–9 concerning his plans to visit Corinth with those of 4:19. There he suggests that he will come shortly, but here he exhibits uncertainty about the exact time of his arrival. In chapter 4 Paul is rebuking those who feel that they can run the church without him. To them he warns, "I'll be there sooner than you think" (Barrett). Here he is soberly describing his movements and presenting a timetable of his activities. The difference in mood will explain the apparent differences in statement.

For Further Study

1. Read the article on "Sabbath" in *The Zondervan Pictorial Bible Dictionary*.

2. Read 2 Corinthians 8 and 9 in comparison with 1 Corinthians 16:1–4. List the principles that Paul uses to motivate Christian giving in all of these passages.

Chapter 11

Conclusion

(1 Corinthians 16:10–24)

In concluding 1 Corinthians Paul makes reference to Timothy and Apollos, both of whom have been previously mentioned in the writing. In 4:17 Paul mentioned that Timothy was en route to Corinth, and here he suggests how he should be received when he appears. Apollos has been mentioned in 1:12; 3:4–5; and 4:6, and Paul provides the latest news from the eloquent disciple for those in Corinth who were eager to see him. In 16:13–18 Paul includes some miscellaneous commands about Christian conduct that summarize and amplify many requests previously made. His final greetings and benediction are similar to those of his other writings, but the numerous personal references contained in Romans are not duplicated here for the Christians in Corinth.

A. General Instructions Concerning Timothy and Apollos (16:10–12)

From Acts 19:22 it seems that Timothy was accompanied by Erastus and that they first went to Macedonia before coming to Corinth. Perhaps Erastus is not mentioned here again because as a Corinthian he would be returning home (Rom. 16:23). The words of verse 10, "if Timothy comes," leave the arrival of Timothy in Corinth as an uncertainty, but the probability that he would arrive there was great. Paul's words indicate a certain uneasiness concerning Timothy's visit to Corinth. Timothy was timid (2 Tim. 1:6,7) and may not have been highly cultivated. He would naturally feel ill at ease among some who did not respect Paul. Paul may have feared that Timothy might be inadequate for dealing with confident, self-willed people, and he commends him to the Corinthians as working the same spiritual work as Paul. Paul demonstrated his significant trust of Timothy by the important responsibilities he assigned to him, and elsewhere he is uncommonly lavish in his praise of this young disciple (Phil. 2:19–24). He was eager that the Corinthians not look on Timothy with disrespect, and he wants them to send him on his way so that he might leave in peace with all of the Corinthian Christians. The NEB says, "Send him happily on his way to join me." The "brothers" mentioned in verse 11 may refer to the three Corinthians in 16:17 who had awaited the arrival of Timothy in Ephesus in order to carry some new instructions or a new letter from Paul back to Corinth.

The manner in which Paul again mentions Apollos in verse 12 suggests that the two disciples were on good terms. They were not conscious of any rivalry between them. The statement that Apollos was "quite unwilling" to come then to Corinth may suggest that he foresaw that the cause of unity in Corinth would best be served by his absence. There is no evidence that Apollos ever again reached Corinth, for he is not mentioned in 2 Corinthians.

B. General Instructions Concerning Christian Conduct (16:13–18)

Paul is now drawing his writing to a close, and he gives five terse commands in verses 13 and 14. To "be on your guard" warns them against surprise spiritual attacks that would exploit their weaknesses. To "stand firm in the faith" can either refer to their holding the true content of the Christian faith or to their demonstrating a true trust in God. To "be men of courage" and to "be strong" calls on the Corinthians to have energy, a subjective disposition, and also real power due to God's divine help, an objective reality. This energy and power were to be directed by love. Four of these commands refer to the spiritual opponents and dangers facing the Corinthians. The fifth reminds them of their duty to one another. The first four commands would be directed respectively against the carelessness, fickleness, immaturity, and moral weakness of the Corinthians.

Paul's words in 16:15–18 commend Stephanas and those who had visited Paul with him. Paul had earlier mentioned (1:16) baptizing the household of Stephanas, and he now adds that they were the firstfruits of the province of Achaia. Since Athens was also a part of this province and Paul had converts there before coming to Corinth (Acts 17:34), the use of the word "first" raises a problem in understanding. Perhaps the household of Stephanas had been converted before Paul preached at Athens. It may also be that there were earlier conversions of individuals at Athens, but this was the first household to be won. It may be that the term shows "those fruits which gave promise of the harvest to come" (Morris). Stephanas and his household had appointed themselves under God to a ministry of service in Corinth. One of the problems in Corinth had been a failure to recognize properly those who were able to lead, and Paul urges the Corinthians to submit to Stephanas and to others who help and toil (v. 16). Function and not an artificial status became the basis of rendering respect and subordination. Those who performed the work were to receive the proper recognition and respect. Discipline rather than unbridled self-expression was to be a feature of the Christian life. Williams captures Paul's words at the beginning of verse 16 when he says, "I beg you to put yourselves under leaders like these." Paul specifically commends Stephanas, Fortunatus, and Achaicus in verse 17. In their coming they had brought to Paul a little taste of Corinth. The men could not have brought good spiritual news about Corinth, but their fellowship and service to Paul must have been refreshing. They brought to him personal fellowship with Corinth that had been lacking. It may also be true that they did bring expressions of love from godly Corinthians (and there were some!) and were able to interpret distressing reports in a less distressing manner. Such reports had refreshed Paul's spirit, and the return of these three would provide a refreshing experience for the Corinthian church. Men like these who could help to cheer Paul and the church in Corinth were to be acknowledged.

Nothing specifically is known of the companions of Stephanas. It was common, however, for a slave to bear a name reflecting the country of his birth. Some feel that Achaicus was born in Achaia and was a slave of Chloe (Godet).

C. Greetings (16:19–20)

The churches of Asia were those founded in Ephesus and other surrounding cities during the time of Paul's ministry there (Acts 19:10). Aquila and Priscilla had come to Corinth from Rome (Acts 18:2), and they left Corinth with Paul for Ephesus (Acts 18:18). In Romans 16:3 they were back in Rome. They had probably risked their lives for Paul in Ephesus (Rom. 16:4), and they had used their home as a meeting place for the church both in Rome (Rom. 16:5) and in Ephesus (v. 19). The custom of kissing as a form of greeting was more widespread in the ancient world than it is in modern Western civilization. The reference here is to a physical expression that would be similar in meaning to the handshake in Western culture. Christian worship services eventually utilized a liturgical kiss of peace, a kiss exchanged during worship, but this practice was introduced much later than the time for the writing of 1 Corinthians.

D. Benediction (16:21–24)

Paul's words in verse 21 were an effort to authenticate his letter. He habitually dictated his letters to a secretary called an amanuensis (Rom. 16:22). By taking the pen and writing a few sections in his own handwriting he verified that the letter was his own (Gal. 6:11; Col. 4:18). Paul would have had little appreciation for someone who used his name pseudonymously in order to circulate his own ideas (2 Thess. 2:2).

Paul had written this letter to a congregation rife with moral laxity and a party spirit. True devotion to the Lord would correct this condition. If anyone finally proved unwilling to render this consecration and devotion to God, Paul declared what his final condemnation would be (v. 22). The term "anathema," or "a curse be on him," refers to a separation from God. Paul is not here saying "good riddance!" to a troublesome unbeliever, but he is pronouncing in advance what the unbeliever can expect from God. "Marana tha" is an Aramaic phrase that most likely means "Our Lord, Come." Its preservation by a congregation of Greek-speaking Christians suggests that the hope of the Lord's return was an early, fervent belief of Christians. It was uttered as a prayer by faithful believers.

Paul concludes his letter with a note of spiritual hope and personal esteem for his converts. He wishes them an experience of God's grace. He again assures them of his love. Despite his frank words in the letter Paul still loved the Corinthians with a deep affection, and his last words are an effort to reassure his readers of that fact.

For Further Study

1. Read the articles on "Kiss," "Apollos," "Priscilla," and "Aquila" in *The Zondervan Pictorial Bible Dictionary*.

2. Read 16:10–24 and then describe actions by you or your church that could encourage deeper bonds of friendship and compassion among Christians.

Bibliography

Arndt, William F. and Gingrich, F. Wilbur. *A Greek-English Lexicon of the New Testament*. Second Edition. Revised and augmented by F. Wilbur Gingrich and Frederick W. Danker from Walter Bauer's Fifth Edition, 1958. Chicago: The University of Chicago Press, 1979.

Barker, Glenn W., Lane, William L., and Michaels, J. Ramsey. *The New Testament Speaks*. New York: Harper and Row, 1969.

Barrett, C. K. *A Commentary on the First Epistle to the Corinthians* in the "Black's New Testament Commentaries." Second edition. London: Adam and Charles Black, 1971.

Bruce, F. F. *1 and 2 Corinthians* in the "New Century Bible." London: Oliphants, 1971.

Bruner, Frederick Dale. *A Theology of the Holy Spirit*. Grand Rapids: Eerdmans, 1970.

Calvin, John. *Commentary on the Epistles of Paul the Apostle to the Corinthians*. Trans. John Pringle. Reprint. Grand Rapids: Baker, 1979.

Craig, Clarence Tucker. *The First Epistle to the Corinthians—Exegesis*, in "The Interpreter's Bible." New York: Abingdon-Cokesbury, 1953.

Edge, Findley. *A Quest for Vitality in Religion*. Nashville: Broadman, 1963.

Edwards, T. C. *A Commentary on the First Epistle to the Corinthians*. London: Hodder and Stoughton, 1903.

Erdman, Charles R. *The First Epistle of Paul to the Corinthians*. Philadelphia: Westminster, 1965.

Findlay, George G. *St. Paul's First Epistle to the Corinthians* in "The Expositor's Greek Testament." Grand Rapids: Eerdmans, n.d.

Fisher, Fred L. *Commentary on 1 and 2 Corinthians*. Waco, Texas: Word, 1975.

Godet, F. *Commentary on the First Epistle of St. Paul to the Corinthians.* 2 vols. Grand Rapids: Zondervan, 1957.

Gould, E. P. *The First Epistle of Paul the Apostle to the Corinthians* in "The American Commentary on the New Testament," Alvah Hovey, ed. Philadelphia: The American Baptist Publication Society, 1887.

Grosheide, F. W. *Commentary on the First Epistle to the Corinthians* in the "New International Commentary on the New Testament." Grand Rapids: Eerdmans, 1953.

Gundry, Robert H. *A Survey of the New Testament.* Rev. ed. Grand Rapids: Zondervan, 1981.

Hillyer, Norman. *1 and 2 Corinthians* in "The New Bible Commentary. Revised." Grand Rapids: Eerdmans, 1970.

Hodge, Charles. *An Exposition of the First Epistle to the Corinthians.* New York: Hodder and Stoughton, 1857.

Hooker, Morna D. "Authority on her head: an examination of 1 Cor. xi.10, NTS X, 1963–64.

Mare, W. Harold. *1 Corinthians* in "The Expositor's Bible Commentary." Grand Rapids: Zondervan, 1976.

Morris, Leon. *The First Epistle of Paul to the Corinthians,* in the "Tyndale New Testament Commentaries." London: Tyndale Press, 1958.

Robertson, Archibald and Plummer, Alfred. *A Critical and Exegetical Commentary on the First Epistle of St. Paul to the Corinthians,* in the "International Critical Commentary," second edition. Edinburgh: T & T Clark, 1914.

Robertson, A. T. *First Corinthians* in "Word Pictures in the New Testament." New York: Harper and Brothers, 1931.

Scroggie, W. Graham. *The Love Life: 1 Corinthians 13.* Grand Rapids: Kregel, n.d.

Stott, John R. W. *The Baptism and Fullness of the Holy Spirit.* Downers Grove, Illinois: InterVarsity Press, 1964.

All Scriptures, unless otherwise identified, are quoted from the *Holy Bible: New International Version* (NIV). New York Bible Society, 1978. Other translations referred to are as follows:

The American Standard Version. Referred to as ASV.

William F. Beck. *The Holy Bible: An American Translation.* New Haven, Missouri: Leader Publishing Company.

The Bible in Basic English. Cambridge: University Press, 1965.

W. J. Conybeare. *The Epistles of Paul: A Translation and Notes.* Reprint Edition. Grand Rapids: Baker Book House, 1958.

Edgar J. Goodspeed. *The New Testament: An American Translation*. Chicago: The University of Chicago Press, 1951.

Good News for Modern Man. The New Testament in Today's English Version. New York: American Bible Society, 1966. Referred to as TEV.

The King James Version. Referred to as KJV.

Ronald Knox. *The New Testament in the Translation of Monsignor Ronald Knox*. New York: Sheed and Ward, Inc., 1944.

The Modern Language Bible. *The New Berkeley Version*. Grand Rapids: Zondervan Publishing House, 1959. Referred to as MLB.

James Moffatt. *The New Testament: A New Translation*. New York: Harper and Brothers, 1950.

Helen Barrett Montgomery. *The New Testament in Modern English*. Valley Forge: Judson Press, n.d.

The New American Standard Bible. LaHabra: The Lockman Foundation, 1960, 1962, 1963. Referred to as NASB.

The New English Bible. Oxford and Cambridge: University Press, 1965. Referred to as NEB.

Olaf M. Norlie. *The New Testament: A New Translation*. Grand Rapids: Zondervan Publishing House, 1961.

J. B. Phillips. *The New Testament in Modern English*. New York: The Macmillan Company, 1962.

J. B. Rotherham. *The Emphasized Bible*. Grand Rapids: Kregel Publications. Reprint Edition, 1967.

The Holy Bible: Revised Standard Version. New York: National Council of Churches of Christ, 1952. Referred to as RSV.

Kenneth N. Taylor. *The Living Bible*. Wheaton, Illinois: Tyndale House Publishers, 1971. Referred to as LB.

The Twentieth Century New Testament: A Translation into Modern English. Chicago: Moody Press, n.d. Referred to as TCNT.

Richard Francis Weymouth. *The New Testament in Modern Speech*. Newly revised by James Alexander Robertson. New York: Harper and Brothers, n.d.

Charles B. Williams. *The New Testament: A Private Translation in the Language of the People*. Chicago: Moody Press, 1949.